Miami
Transformed

University of Pennsylvania Press Philadelphia

Manny Diaz

Foreword by Michael Bloomberg

Miami
Transformed

Rebuilding America
One Neighborhood, One City at a Time

THE CITY IN THE TWENTY-FIRST CENTURY
Eugenie L. Birch and Susan M. Wachter, Series Editors
Published in collaboration with the Penn Institute for Urban Research

Copyright © 2013 University of Pennsylvania Press

Published by
University of Pennsylvania Press
Philadelphia, Pennsylvania 19104-4112
www.upenn.edu/pennpress

Printed in the United States of America on acid-free paper
10 9 8 7 6 5 4 3 2 1

Library of Congress Cataloging-in-Publication Data
Diaz, Manny.
    Miami transformed : rebuilding America one neighborhood, one city at a time /
Manny Diaz ; foreword by Michael Bloomberg. — 1st ed.
        p.   cm. — (The city in the twenty-first century)
    ISBN 978-0-8122-4464-9 (hardcover : alk. paper)
    Includes bibliographical references and index.
    1. Diaz, Manny. 2. Mayors—Florida—Miami—Biography. 3. Cuban Americans—
Florida—Miami—Biography. 4. Miami (Fla.)—Politics and government—21st century.
5. Miami (Fla.)—Social conditions—21st century. 6. Miami (Fla.)—Economic
conditions—21st century. I. Bloomberg, Michael. I. Title. II. Series: The city in the
twenty-first century
F319.M6 D48   2013
975.9'381   2012029839

Make no little plans; they have no magic to stir men's blood and probably themselves will not be realized.

Make big plans; aim high in hope and work, remembering that a noble diagram once recorded will never die, but long after we are gone will be a living thing.

—Daniel Hudson Burnham, architect and urban planner

Contents

Foreword **Michael Bloomberg**

W E NEED MORE elected officials like Manny Diaz. When Manny was first elected Mayor of Miami, he entered office with the single most important asset any new mayor can have: ignorance. He didn't know what he couldn't do. Those who spend their lives in politics learn to live by certain limitations: groups that cannot be challenged, laws that cannot be changed, projects that cannot be undertaken, words that cannot be uttered. Manny had spent his career in the private sector, and he brought none of this baggage with him. When people wise in the way of government told him one of his ideas could not be achieved, he asked a very simple, and very powerful, question: "Why not?"

This book is for everyone who asks that same question about local, state, or federal government. Why can't government be more efficient and effective? Why can't government get big things done? Why can't government be as innovative and dynamic as the private sector? The answer is: it can. But it takes leaders like Manny Diaz to make it happen.

On issue after issue, Mayor Diaz changed the way Miami city government approached long-standing problems. Instead of seeing poverty as inevitable, he saw it as an area where investments needed to be better targeted. Instead of lamenting the middle class exodus to the suburbs, he saw that residents were "voting with their feet" and needed to be convinced to come back to a city that cared about improving services. Instead of blaming failing schools on the bureaucracy, he led the charge to increase mayoral control. And instead of bemoaning traffic congestion, he advocated for expanded mass transit. Manny Diaz never stopped asking "Why not?" And the innovative approaches he pioneered helped Miami become a national leader on issues that will define the future of our country.

I've had the pleasure of working with and getting to know Manny Diaz over the past decade. We were both first elected to office in November 2001. Both of us had spent our careers in the private sector. And both of us entered government with a philosophy based on pragmatism, not ideology.

Unlike members of Congress, mayors don't have the luxury of spending their days holding ideological debates. We are elected to solve problems that affect people's everyday lives—from fighting crime to fixing potholes. Neither of us believes that, when it comes to governing and public policy, one party has a monopoly on good ideas or truth. As New York Mayor Fiorello La Guardia said in the 1930s, "There is no Democratic or Republican way to pick up the trash." That is still true today. The problem is that now, both parties spend more time maneuvering around problems—in order to position themselves to win the next election—than they do fixing them.

Mayor Diaz and I both became Independents because we saw how, all too often, partisanship stands in the way of progress. The fact is, members of the two parties agree on far more than they admit. But for self-serving political reasons, they would rather engage in combat than collaboration. By and large, mayors put aside partisan differences to find common ground on the most important issues—and few have done it as effectively as Manny Diaz. This book is not only a great American success story—Manny is the son of immigrants who worked his way to the top—but it is also a valuable lesson in the art of pragmatic politics.

Many of the issues I've worked on with Manny have been ones that produce mostly gridlock in Washington—including the most urgent, illegal guns. In 2006, we launched a bi-partisan coalition of Mayors Against Illegal Guns, which today has over 600 members around the country. As President of the U.S. Conference of Mayors, Manny was instrumental in helping the coalition grow—and helping us recruit Democratic, Republican, and Independent mayors. When it comes to illegal guns, both parties in Washington are beholden to special interests—and paralyzed by the fear that talking about the issue will hurt their reelection chances. But mayors see the deadly consequences of illegal guns every day—and we have an obligation to act.

The first responsibility of any mayor is to protect public safety. And mayors owe our police officers—and their families—our commitment to do everything possible to keep illegal guns off the streets. The vast majority of crimes committed with guns are committed by people—felons or the mentally ill—who are not legally allowed to possess a gun. The message that our mayors' coalition has brought to Washington is simple: enforce the laws preventing criminals and the mentally ill from getting guns. It's a message that more than 80 percent of gun owners agree with. Washington, however, remains more interested in ideological debates than pragmatic steps to enforce the law that would save lives.

Although illegal guns are a national problem, mayors understand that we cannot wait for Washington to act. And in Miami, Mayor Diaz refused to allow key public safety matters to be driven by local politics. Despite local opposition, he conducted a national search for a police chief, and ended up hiring one of New York's Finest: John Timoney. During Mayor Diaz's tenure, crime fell dramatically in Miami, with the homicide rate dropping 76 percent from its highest point (similar to what we saw happen in New York). Only a few U.S. cities experienced a greater decrease in crime during the last decade.

Driving down crime is just one area where the mayor refused to allow the gridlock in Washington to prevent local action. For example, while very little is happening to address climate change in our nation's capital, cities are leading the way. Under Mayor Diaz, Miami became a leader in the green buildings movement. And when I was in Miami a few years ago, I got a first-hand look at some of the public transit solutions Mayor Diaz had championed. They not only helped improved people's commuting time, but helped reduce pollution too.

On issue after issue, Mayor Diaz brought an entrepreneurial spirit to Miami's City Hall—and in New York City we were glad to be his partner on many initiatives. Together, we convinced the federal government to create an Urban Innovation Fund to support forward-thinking, hard-hitting antipoverty programs like New York's Center for Economic Opportunity and ACCESS Miami. As members of the Cities for Financial Empowerment coalition, we've worked to find new ways to help low-income families stabilize their finances and savings. When Mayor Diaz started the Mayors' Alliance for Green Schools with Seattle Mayor Greg Nickels, New York signed on as a member. And when Mayor Diaz helped led the charge for nonpartisan redistricting—so that legislative districts are not carved up to protect incumbents—I gladly lent my support.

This openness to collaboration also led Mayor Diaz to form partnerships with the private sector on many critical local issues. Government cannot accomplish everything by itself, but that is no excuse for inaction. Through public-private partnerships, mayors can invest in neighborhoods, tackle difficult social problems, and spur economic growth. In New York, these partnerships have been critical to our success in a wide variety of areas—from revitalizing parks to launching incubators for small businesses to fighting poverty. In Miami, Manny leveraged public-private partnerships to improve the quality of life for residents—and attract billions of dollars in new investment. By making Miami an even more powerful magnet for residents and visitors, he made it an even more powerful magnet for businesses looking to expand and grow.

Manny Diaz was a great mayor, and he will go down in history as one of our country's most innovative urban leaders because he put progress before partisanship—and because he never stopped asking, "Why not?" His legacy will be defined not only by a soaring skyline, but also by cutting-edge policies that made Miami a national leader on urban issues. That work will not only benefit Miami for generations to come: it will influence cities around the country and the world. Now more than ever, not only are cities competing with each other in a global marketplace; we are learning from one another. And as you will read in these pages, there is a great deal to learn from Manny Diaz's experience in Miami.

Miami
Transformed

I WROTE THIS BOOK because the focus of politics in America has to change.

Many politicians write memoirs and biographies, filled with anecdotes and personal recollections from their term in office. There is a lot of that in these pages. It is also my hope that you will find something much more important. My premise is that we need to restore pragmatism in politics through a renewed investment in our cities. Unless we do so, we will continue to head down a very perilous road.

I understand I am not the first to say this. Yet, it is a painful realization. This is especially true given my background: born in another country, a political exile in the United States, the country that took me in, where I grew up and came to deeply appreciate and love the liberty and boundless opportunity this nation provides. My personal and professional experience—from immigrant, to businessman, to mayor of a major American city—have brought me to this conclusion: to rebuild America, we must rebuild our cities, making investments in the people and places that make us great, and make us who we are.

□ □ □

I HAVE SPENT my life as an observer and student of politics, from high school class president to serving as mayor of Miami for eight years, but I've never seen the political landscape as bad as it is now. What we need is a return to basics, a return to cities, to the political unit closest to the people. Life has taught me that history is always about choices, those moments and defining times when one can take a path that leads to a conclusion. A true leader can help you understand and make those choices. What path are we on now?

We've all heard the dire statistics. But in America, no matter how bad things have been, there has always been hope for the future, that the next generation would be better off. Our national forebears forged a revolution, survived a Civil War, fought two World Wars, defeated fascism and communism, and brought the advent of gender and racial equality, always believing the hope and promise of this nation—that tomorrow would always be better. This idea makes us the only country in the world that inspires a "Dream." It was a phrase coined in the early part of the last century during the Great Depression—the American Dream—a land in which life should be better, richer, and fuller for everyone with opportunity for all.

Measuring ourselves by the ancient Athenian Pledge—*to transmit this country greater, better, stronger, prouder and more beautiful than it was transmitted to us*—Where does that leave us? We are failing by all accounts. According to recent census figures, over 140 million Americans have fallen into poverty or are scraping by on earnings that classify them as low income. And how many people do you know who, in spite of having jobs and working hard, are living paycheck to paycheck, unable to save for college or retirement? Most troubling, the national mood indicates that a majority of Americans generally feel our best days are behind us.

Meanwhile, the world continues to catch up to us. As a nation, we now live in a world where information travels around the globe in a millisecond. The information age has indeed made the world "flat."

Localities must now have a competitive advantage. In today's world, businesses have a great deal of choice as to where they invest and create jobs. This is especially true in today's global economy, where corporations no longer owe an allegiance to any one nation, nor are they tied to any one location.

Much is made of the "outsourcing" of U.S. jobs, and politicians are quick to offer sound bite opinions on this, but no one asks: Why do corporations and investors choose one place over another? When we see corporations shipping jobs and investments overseas, we have a right to be angry. But instead of stoking this anger for political gain, we must also ask why these decisions were made. What prompted them to do this in the first place? What has made investment in the U.S. so unattractive that this company went elsewhere? And how can we make it stop—how do we become competitive again?

There are some who will always believe the United States will be number one no matter what. Our future is not guaranteed. Many other nations are pushing the frontiers of progress; they are looking inward and not afraid to invest in themselves and their people. The twentieth century saw the end of European dominance; this could be the century where America loses its dominance.

World powers today compete for economic strength and the weapons are not nuclear or missiles: the weapons are information and currency. Indeed, there is a trend for younger, well-educated workers to leave the United States in search of opportunities in other countries. Our immigration policies are such that while many of the world's best brains study in our colleges and universities, we are unable to retain them. Every dollar we don't spend, or worse yet misspend, every failure to invest, leads to more confidence lost, putting others around the world one step closer to catching and beating us. Countries like China, Russia, India, and Brazil are gaining on us by investing in their cities and people. They are also buying us out. In the past decade, our foreign debt has skyrocketed, with China holding the greatest portion of our debt. Other countries have figured out that it is easier to buy us than to bomb us.

We have a multi-trillion-dollar deficit without a foundation that can sustain our continued appetite for spending, placing us on the road from being the world's greatest power to becoming the world's greatest borrower. At the same time, our continued crumbling infrastructure places us at a competitive disadvantage.

While much of the attention of our politics remains focused on the national level and inside the Beltway, ideas and solutions are not coming from Washington, D.C. The economic policies of past administrations have eroded the middle class. The competing theories of "trickle down" and spending that perpetuate dependency have not worked. Much in the same way that when business stops spending, the economy stops growing and jobs are lost, government cannot cut its way back to prosperity. On the other hand, an absolute safety net of dependency is simply not sustainable.

Government is not the end all and be all, nor is it altogether unnecessary. Government has a role—to create, through investment, the climate of opportunity and attraction, where people and business will then invest, either through capital or by choosing to live in one place over another. Let me make something very clear: there is a great difference between investing and spending. Investments have a clear aim and an expected return, mere spending does not. Government investments, therefore, must be targeted and strategic, leading to greater returns.

Much in the same way, business always needs to innovate to maintain a competitive edge and survive, so must government—and it must begin in the place where it has the most impact, in our cities. To survive as a nation, we must ensure that our cities remain competitive. It is time we end the focus on D.C. and Beltway based solutions, and return to a focus on our cities.

Currently, the world is experiencing a renewed urbanization. Over 50 percent of the world's population now live in cities, with the number being over 80 percent for the United States. Metro areas drive our national economy, accounting for 92 percent of the nation's economic growth, almost 90 percent of all jobs, income, and Gross Domestic Product. Cities, therefore, have the most impact on our people. They are where we as a nation can realize the greatest return on our investment. In the chapters that follow, you will see examples of how focused investments in five key areas—(expansion of economic opportunity/public safety/infrastructure/ sustainability/arts/culture) took Miami from a city that was once known as a laughingstock and transformed it into the face of the new American city.

□ □ □

I STILL REMEMBER a 1981 cover from *Time* Magazine declaring that Miami was "Paradise Lost." The article cited how Miami ranked number one on the FBI list of most crime ridden cities in America and that an "estimated 70 percent of all marijuana and cocaine imported into the U.S." came in through South Florida. *Scarface* and *Miami Vice* are what people saw in movies and on television. The prevalence of "Cocaine Cowboys," race riots, and other negative factors added to the reputation of Miami: that it was a nice place to visit, briefly, but not a place to raise your children, start a business, or call home.

Our politics were also chaotic, with a mayoral election nullified due to fraud and a judge choosing the mayor. The city had highest tax rate possible, with little to show in return for the money it collected from its residents. In fact, the city was in so much debt that when I took office it had been bankrupt and placed under state supervision and control. There was even a referendum calling for the dissolution of the city; people had literally given up.

Any growth in the city happened in spite of itself, an accident of weather and geography rather than any concerted planning or leadership. The excuse from city leaders was that "Miami has weather and water, investors will come." But the money was going elsewhere. People, investors, and businesses were not moving into the city, but moving out, leaving in droves. If, as the old saying goes, "people vote with their feet," the only footsteps heard in Miami were those of people too poor to leave for the suburbs.

This hurt me personally. Miami is the city I grew up in, where my parents and so many others like them found refuge. It is where I went to school and worked as a professional, and it was and still is my home. I knew that Miami had great potential, great people, but we needed a plan of action to change the course of the city. In order to survive, Miami had to become attractive and competitive once again.

Competition is something I loved, something I learned from sports, and something I translated to politics and my term as mayor. My goal was to make Miami attractive to investors and businesses—attractive to people looking for a place to live and a city to call home. How did we make this happen? Government began to invest in the people, places, and things that create a climate of attraction for people and business.

First, government must act as a partner: not a solution, not a hindrance. Next, you invest in the things that create a sense of place, the things that make a place worth living.

Take Downtown Miami, for example. No major building had gone up in more than twenty years prior to my administration. It had zero residential life, and became a ghost town after five o'clock. So I sat down with Jorge Pérez, a friend and real estate developer. Jorge told me he would not build a single family home in Miami, much less a major project, because government in Miami simply didn't care about the way downtown looked and operated. If City Hall doesn't invest in the neighborhood, why should he?

I told him things were going to change, and they did. We began to invest in all our neighborhoods, doing the things citizens should expect from their government. We put money into safety, infrastructure, the arts, picking up the garbage, fixing the streets, making our city livable once again. We would call it "Safe, clean, and green!"

Aware of our plans to build a baywalk that would extend for miles on our bay front, Jorge decided to test our resolve, to determine whether our words would match our actions. Prior to moving forward on his first project, Jorge set one condition: that we build a $4 million baywalk lined with beautiful art in the area abutting the project. We agreed. As a result, Jorge built One Miami, the first residential project in Downtown Miami in decades. He would become one of the largest real estate developers in Miami and among the largest in the world.

Having worked in the private sector all my life, I knew that developers (and for that matter, most businesses) are hesitant to be pioneers. However, time and time again, I had witnessed what happens when you convince one prominent pioneer to lead the way: others quickly follow. And follow they did. Our initial investment produced a private sector explosion to the tune of tens of billions of dollars, a threefold increase in our tax base, and a skyline rated third best in the United States, trailing only New York and Chicago. Government kept its word, made the initial investment, and the private sector followed.

Midtown Miami is another example. What was an abandoned 56 acre railyard full of prostitutes and crack dealers when I took office became a multi-billion-dollar project housing one of the fastest growing residential neighborhoods in the city. Its success has spilled over into other once neglected neighborhoods, Wynwood and the Design District. This time a New York developer, Joe Cayre, would serve as the pioneer in an area of the city where district commissioner Johnny Winton and I had failed to convince any local developer to invest. Prior to going "hard" (that is, nonrefundable) on his purchase deposit, Joe also tested our commitment. Once convinced that we would deliver on our promises to expedite the project and invest in its infrastructure, he looked me in the eye, shook my hand, and the rest is history.

This would repeat itself throughout the entire city, including the story of investor Lev Leviev and the Africa Israel investment group, whose land assemblage will one day become a multi-billion-dollar project known as the Miami World Center, to be developed by Art Falcone, Nitin Motwani, and their investment group. Why? Government invested in these areas. We cleaned them up, built new roads and infrastructure, and made them safe. Private investment then followed. For every dollar the city put in, we got and continue to receive exponential returns.

□ □ □

GOVERNMENT NEEDS TO go back to the principles of making targeted investment in the people and things that will yield results. When you invest in people—through education, job training, the arts, health, public safety—you develop a citizenry that is educated and prepared to compete with the best and brightest in the world. They may even grow up to become mayor of a major metropolitan city.

When you invest in place—through better infrastructure that includes bridges, roads, ports, and technology—you create the kind of communities where private investment follows, and that people are proud to call home. As a country, we need to set aside differences and instead have a conversation about our shared priorities. Where do we as Americans need to invest in order to get the best possible results? The answer: in our cities. Let us agree on our priorities, fund them, invest in our people and places, then get out of the way and let America's entrepreneurial spirit take over.

This is the lesson you learn as a mayor—when one minute you are meeting with a Fortune 500 CEO and the next minute you have a lady in your office who has a pothole in her street. Every person matters. Every problem is important to the person who faces that problem. Government's role is to create the climate where both the CEO and the lady are confident that government is reactive and responsive to their needs, where government has made an investment for their success. It is a lesson that worked for Miami, one that can work for our nation as well.

I

T BEGAN AS a fairly typical morning for me—a typical morning for any six-year-old child in Cuba. I awoke to the beautiful sunny skies of Havana, "La Habana," and sat down for a breakfast of "café con leche"—coffee with milk—and bread. At the table sat my mother, Elisa, and maternal grandparents, Benigno and Hortensia Galnares, as the traditional Cuban home very often included several generations under the same roof.

But this was not to be a typical morning.

My father, Manolo, would start his day as a political prisoner in possibly the worst Cuban prison of its time: "La Cabaña." Several of his friends had been executed at the "Paredón," a massive wall covered in the blood of those killed, and my father's fate was yet to be decided. That day we were joined by my paternal grandparents, Manolo, Sr., and Lucía, who also dropped in for breakfast. My grandfather would not stop crying and I had no idea why. It would be the last time I ever saw him. It would also be my last day on Cuban soil. Mom told me that because Dad was in prison, it was probably best if I spent the summer vacationing in Miami with aunt Aida, uncle Benigno, and cousins Lena, Julio, and Alex Galnares. So, after breakfast, we drove to José Martí Airport for my first plane ride, a late morning Pan Am flight to Miami.

At the airport, my mother was approached by one of Fidel Castro's militia members, a *miliciano*, and was told that my seat on the flight had been sold for $500 to another passenger. My mother now believed we would never be allowed to leave Cuba. The *miliciano* ordered us to wait in a glass-enclosed area of the airport known as "La Pecera," the Fishbowl. While I sat there, I could see my grandparents on the other side of the glass, crying. They cried, my mom cried, I cried. Finally, the *miliciano* returned to tell my mom that we could board the plane, but I would have to sit on her lap during the flight. We were the last to board.

When our plane finally took off, my mother started to cry again. She cried the entire flight. She would never again set foot in her country of birth. I can only now imagine the worries she felt, separated from her husband and family, wondering if she would ever see them again. And what fears, starting a new life with her six-year-old son in a foreign country, only a dime in her pocket (so she could phone my uncle when we landed), and enough clothes to last a few days.

We landed in Miami in mid-afternoon. My uncle met us at the airport and drove us to his small apartment in Little Havana. (Forty years later, I would open the headquarters for my mayoral campaign just two blocks from my first home in America.) We all had some more café con leche and bread—now called Cuban bread in Miami—and the eight of us went to sleep, not knowing the fate that awaited us all.

It was indeed a typical day that July 21, 1961: a day I will never forget. It changed the course of my family. Like other Cuban families in exile, we were bound by the hope that one day soon, we would return to celebrate true freedom and independence for our homeland. Every single year since, my mom calls me on July 21 to remind me that this is the day we left Cuba to start our new lives in our new country. It would be a year and a half before I saw my father again.

◻ ◻ ◻

MY FATHER'S FAMILY was very poor.

Fulgencio Batista, Castro's predecessor, is credited with investing a tremendous amount of money in infrastructure and education. In the late 1930s, Batista built vocational boarding schools for poor children throughout Cuba. For the inaugural class, the government chose 250 of the poorest students on the island to attend. My dad was one of them. After graduating from the vocational school, he worked as a physical education instructor at a school where the administrator's daughter taught first grade. That's how my mom and dad met.

I was born in Havana a year later in a clinic. Cuba had the precursor of what we now know as Health Maintenance Organizations, or HMOs. My parents would pay a flat rate of approximately $2.50 a month for services, from the delivery of a child to brain surgery.

In 1959 our lives changed dramatically when Fidel Castro came down from the hills and ousted Batista. My mom and dad were not political—although, in a way, every Cuban is political. They love to talk about politics and are very passionate about it, but they were not active in any political party or cause.

My dad, however, quickly ended up in prison as an enemy of the state. After Castro nationalized the electric utility, my dad, an employee of the utility and a member of the electrical workers union, formed part of a group that organized and conducted a strike, refusing to work for Castro. He also secretly helped several friends find safe haven in foreign embassies, facilitating their escape from Cuba. For these activities, he was thrown in jail as a political prisoner.

His prison term was served in "La Cabaña," within the Morro Castle, and possibly the worst prison of its time in Cuba. My dad was lucky: after nearly two years, a friend "paid" the authorities to release him. Most of his union colleagues were not so lucky—they were executed at the Paredón.

Mom would regularly take dad food. On her way to see him, the guards would purposely escort her through the Paredón, where she would be forced to walk over the fresh blood of those who had recently been executed. Often, as she walked past the Paredón, the guards would carry out a mock execution, shooting blanks at the men lined up against the wall. In an effort to further humiliate her, they would randomly strip-search her. The guards would keep whatever they wanted from the care packages she intended for my dad. After the failed Bay of Pigs invasion in 1961, my mom was no longer allowed to enter the prison during her visits. She could only speak to my dad from outside the prison fence.

My dad begged my mother to take me out of Cuba. Rumors had begun to spread that the government was taking kids from families to work camps to cut sugarcane. It is important to understand that under the Cuban constitution as revised by Castro, parental rights are nonexistent. Children are wards of the state, and the state can determine where they go. This concept is difficult to understand, and almost impossible to relate to, by those of us who have been raised in America. As such, its real significance was lost on many in America during the Elián González debate (something I will address later in this book).

My father wanted me out of Cuba. Understandably, my mom did not want to leave her husband's side, not knowing if she would ever see him again, not knowing if he would end up executed like so many of his friends. This difficult conflict, common to so many Cuban parents, even led my dad to threaten her with divorce if his wish (perhaps his last) for his son was not honored. My mother honored my father's wish. This is why I left Cuba to join my uncle's family for a "summer vacation" in Miami.

◻ ◻ ◻

MY AUNT AND UNCLE, my three cousins, and my uncle's mother-in-law all lived in a small apartment in Little Havana. There were only two bedrooms, so my mom and I had to sleep on the sofa in the living room. During this time there was one day I will never forget. In those early years, there were no Spanish language radio or television stations, a fact that may seem hard to believe for some today. However, one local radio station broadcast in Spanish for a couple of hours every afternoon. Much of the broadcast was dedicated to reading the names of the Cuban prisoners who had been executed by the Castro government. One day, while playing outside with my cousins, we heard screaming and crying from within the apartment. Obviously something was terribly wrong, and watching our parents cry we too began to cry, not really knowing why. It turned out that one of the names announced that afternoon was Manuel Diaz. We believed my father had been executed. Fortunately, after much effort and despair, my mother was able to place a call to family in Cuba who confirmed he had not been executed.

Thankfully, my father joined us at the end of 1962. Because of his "counter-revolutionary" activities, Castro's government refused to issue him an exit visa. Nevertheless, my mother was able to secure a "fake" visa. Apparently, someone in the family had a relationship with a Cuban government official, and probably paid to obtain the visa that allowed him to enter the United States. I was also able to be reunited with my grandparents. In fact, my grandparents always lived with us, maintaining the long-standing tradition of multiple generations living in the same home. With my parents forced to hold several jobs at a time to make ends meet, my grandparents played a major role in my formative years.

I became very close to my grandfather. He had a huge influence on my life. While not a political person, as an educator he was very active in promoting educational opportunities for all Cubans. To this day, I am regularly approached by so many people in Miami whose lives he had touched in his beloved town of Regla, always eager to share with me just how much they loved and admired him. I truly enjoyed hearing his stories and understanding his perspective on life, politics, and his beloved country. I was particularly impressed with his ability to keep an open mind on issues. That was especially noteworthy growing up the way I did in a community of people who had just received the shock—and what greater shock can there be other than death?—of being uprooted completely from your way of life. It was important for him that I use his life's experience not to become bitter or angry, but rather to fully understand the underlying reasons for the events that would shape my own future. No doubt he was sad; no doubt he had plenty of reason to be bitter and angry; but now, looking back on those years, it is clear to me that he wanted something more for his first grandchild.

He was an idealist who opposed all forms of dictatorship. He was never a Batista supporter, and resented the multiple coups and the corruption so prevalent in Cuban politics. He was intensely honest and a strong advocate for providing educational opportunities and human rights for all people.

We continued to live with my uncle's family until my dad arrived. We then moved into an even smaller apartment just a couple of blocks away in Little Havana. The apartment is still there and I often drive by to see it, by myself or with my family, as a reminder about where it all started. One of those visits occurred during my mayoral campaign; this time I introduced myself to the current tenants and explained that this is where I had first lived in Miami. They were, of course, an immigrant family, but not Cuban. Little Havana has become the "Little" capital for a number of Latin American and Caribbean countries. Because Miami continues to be the entry point for so many in search of the American Dream, immigrants from all over the Americas, not just Cuba, now call Miami home.

Immediately after his arrival, my dad went to work. He parked cars and worked as a busboy and a dishwasher. A proud man, I remember vividly the stories of how he would have to run in the pouring rain to retrieve a car only to be tipped a nickel—a tip he would refuse. Though very poor (and soaking wet), his sense of integrity would not be compromised by others who held him in such low regard. Few things would anger him more than to see a person treated with anything other than the respect any human being deserved, rich or poor. He would later find work at a bed manufacturing company, where he accidentally cut off a portion of one of his fingers, and spent the balance of his years working in a series of factories and warehouses.

When we first arrived in Miami, my mom could only find work cleaning houses. Subsequently, she worked in a wholesale book warehouse in Liberty City in Miami. She would ride a bus to and from work every day. Practically all her coworkers were black, and to this day she reminds me of how fond she was of them. They befriended her, walking her to the bus stop and waiting for her bus to arrive. For years, she maintained a very close personal relationship with one of them. Despite the efforts of many in the community, including the media, to foster divisions between blacks and new immigrants, I have always found very little division when there is person-to-person contact. For it is not color or language that divides us, but economic status and dreams for our families that unite us.

After some time, my dad secured a job at an auto parts factory. Because they could only afford one car, my mom also got a job at the same factory doing clerical work.

I grew up in Little Havana and began my education at my neighborhood school, Shenandoah Elementary. In Cuba, I had been enrolled in a bilingual school. Morning classes were taught in English, afternoon classes in Spanish, or vice versa. Regrettably, we have a very parochial notion about language in our country—how we're all supposed to forget whatever language we (or our ancestors) used to speak, and speak only English. When you travel the world, it's often different; people are encouraged to learn the language not just of their country but of others as well. But we Americans expect everyone to speak English.

Shenandoah was not predominantly Cuban. My memories of recess involved a ritual: fighting with the American kids. We would go out to the school yard; the Cuban kids would form one line and the American kids would form another line. For reasons yet unknown, we would fight during the entire recess (or until someone stopped the fight). We did not need a reason. It was just simply a ritual.

Elementary school was fairly uneventful. I did well, picking up English rather quickly; in fact, most of us did. It would bother some of the American kids that we would win spelling bees. "You just got off the boat, what are you doing winning a spelling bee?" they would ask incredulously. Our parents taught us to work hard, study hard, learn English, and that in the United States everything is possible. My focus during my elementary school years, however, was baseball. I would wake up in the morning and fall asleep at night with a ball in my hand. It was my love.

☐ ☐ ☐

IN 1967, as sixth grade was ending, I was selected to play on a baseball team that had been invited to participate in the Bronco division of the Boys' League World Championship. Our team, made up exclusively of young Cubans, would be called Miami Cuba Libre (Free Cuba). No one had given us much of a chance to win. Because the tournaments were double elimination (if you lose two games, you are eliminated), most people thought we would be back in Miami quickly. As a result, my parents packed two sets of everything for me: a couple of pairs of underwear, a couple of t-shirts. They gave me five dollars, kissed me goodbye, and expected me to return home in two days. Much to everyone's surprise, we were away practically the entire month of August. We had to keep calling for more underwear, and a little more money.

The games took us from Alabama to Texas. It was the first time I was truly exposed to the rest of America. Up to that point, I lived mainly in an immigrant environment, surrounded by the smells of Cuban food and listening to the beat of Cuban music. Clearly, I was dealing with kids in school who were not Cuban—even though I was apparently fighting them most of the time! Some of my non-Cuban classmates did live in the same neighborhood, but I wasn't being invited over to Johnny's house for meatloaf and mashed potatoes. So the baseball tour exposed me to a larger view of America. When I look back, I'm struck that it was 1967 and there I was in Birmingham, Alabama, playing baseball in close proximity to Dr. King's march for justice and equality.

We stayed at the homes of our host teams. As a result, I learned that Americans had eggs and ham or bacon and muffins for breakfast. This was a real culture shock. In my family, breakfast consisted of just coffee with milk and Cuban toast—that's it. What I was eating for breakfast in those homes in Alabama was what we would be lucky to have for dinner at my house. I remember laughing with my parents afterward, saying, "I love these Americans, they sure know how to eat breakfast." Little did I know that I was putting them in an awkward spot. "Well son, we'd love to feed you that way too, but we just can't afford it." To this day, breakfast continues to be my favorite meal. It still consists of café con leche and Cuban toast, but it also includes eggs and ham, the best of both worlds.

Traveling with my team did a lot to expand my horizons, not just when it came to food. After playing and winning in Birmingham, we went to Kingsville, Texas, for the finals. Kingsville had a large Mexican American population that welcomed us with open arms. Because we spoke Spanish and had a strong sense of pride in our shared cultural heritage, they absolutely fell in love with us and we with them: we became "their" team. They would show up at our games, and invite us for barbecues after the game. For us, it was like, "Hey, they are just like us!"

These are the kinds of experiences that helped shape who I am today. I learned that too often people will hold opinions of others on the basis of something they have heard or read. They allow themselves to become critical of others because they sound or look different. We are all products of our own experiences in life. Regrettably, those experiences generally do not include personal exposure to other people and cultures. Traveling to Alabama and Texas did that for me, making me a better person. It also led to my future involvement in the fight for civil rights, the rights of farmworkers, and the plight of all immigrants.

By the time we reached the finals in Kingsville, our games were being broadcast in Miami in Spanish, and the local Spanish newspaper even sent a reporter to cover the finals. The games had become so popular with the local community that some estimated attendance at 10,000. Included among those attending were professional baseball scouts. We ended up undefeated, and in the process became world champions. Incidentally, in the final series game, with our team trailing 1 to 0, I hit a game-winning two-run homer.

Back home in Little Havana, our team became the rallying cry for a community desperate for some good news. On our return from Texas, thousands at Miami International Airport welcomed us. We left the airport in used Cadillac convertibles (the father of one the players ran a used car lot), and were given a ticker tape parade through Little Havana. We rode up and down Southwest Eighth Street and Flagler Street several times. During the weeks that followed, we were honored by almost every Cuban exile organization of its day, were given a key to the City of Miami, and appeared on local English language television stations. It was the Cuban community's proudest moment during the early exile years.

This was 1967. Most of us had only been here five, six, seven years. Many in the community were still washing dishes, still struggling. There was no good news from Cuba, no prospect for a quick return, until suddenly this group of kids out of nowhere became world champions. I continued to play baseball in high school, both for the school team and for summer and evening leagues. I dreamed of playing baseball professionally; to become the Cuban Mickey Mantle. But this was very difficult for Cuban kids in my era. We had two obstacles. One was economic. Most of us had to start working at an early age in order to help our parents.

The other obstacle that set back many young people during those years was drugs. It was one or the other. As I grew older and still played ball, you could begin to see a difference with the next wave of young Cuban Americans. Although younger, this group was close enough in age that we were in the same field together. Many of them went on to play college and professional baseball. Why? One reason was time. I would go to a park and see them practicing with their fathers. We were not so lucky. Our fathers were working two or three jobs and we were working too. If your father can spare the afternoon and go out with you to a park, you can continue to develop your skills. None of us had that opportunity. It was: I have to go to school and then I'm going to work. Either I dedicate myself to school and make sure that I have the grades to get into college, or I take a chance and hope to pitch in the Major Leagues someday. I chose college and law school.

We did, of course, have time for fun. My dad was very social; he loved to have people over at our house all the time. There was always some sort of gathering, a party, a barbecue on weekends. In those days, as a host, you simply couldn't afford to supply steaks or hamburgers for everyone. Instead, guests would show up with their meal in a package and place it on the grill.

We also spent a lot of time on the beach. The beach is free. That's one of the true benefits of living in a place like Miami: nature is free. All you had to do is pack yourself a ham sandwich, a Cawy (Cuban soda) and make a whole day out of it. Parks were important too. Because of baseball, I spent all my spare time in parks: all day Saturday, Sunday, and after school when I was finished my homework. Of course, my grandfather would drive me to and from the park. Parks were my second home, and kept me out of trouble. Had that outlet not been available, who knows? When you're a kid and you're idle, you're influenced by your peers, and many of mine ended up taking the wrong road. My best friend in elementary school, who also happened to live across the street from me, would go on to become one of the most infamous drug dealers in

America. Still, growing up in my type of environment, you have to learn to live and protect yourself on the streets.

□ □ □

MONEY WAS A RECURRING issue for my family. While growing up, we were forced to move several times, all within Little Havana. I remember the dinnertime conversation: "They've just raised our rent twenty-five dollars a month, so we have to find another place." Imagine that: a twenty-five-dollar increase and we had to pack up. It was more than they could afford. With a very limited income, any increase was hard. Fortunately, our landlords were decent people; they understood my parents' plight and tried to work with them as much as possible. They were not trying to take advantage of my parents, but increases are inevitable: taxes go up; the cost of living goes up. This is why, a year after I graduated from law school, I bought my parents their first house. I surprised my mother on her birthday with a warranty deed to the new house. Thirty years later, she still lives in the same house. She has never had to move again.

Although we were poor, poverty was not a status that dominated my formative years. In fact, I never really understood the fact that I was poor. We had a very happy home life. We were proud of what little we had and took great care to protect it. We blamed no one for our circumstance and believed that being poor was not a lifelong condition, but one of life's challenges that we or anyone in America could overcome. I never heard my parents complain.

Through all this, my parents always emphasized education. My dad especially would drive this point home to me when I worked with him at the auto parts warehouse. We would fill orders for auto parts retailers, who were buying alternators and carburetors—nearly any car part you can imagine—and pack those parts in boxes, many of which were extremely heavy. This did not present a challenge for me. I was young, playing sports and in good physical shape. I enjoyed the additional exercise. But my father? There he was, every day, packing and picking up these boxes. He would always say to me, "You don't want to do this the rest of your life; it's not where you want to be. You have got to stay in school. The only way you're going to move ahead in America is through education. No one will ever be able to take that away from you." He understood the value of education. All our parents did.

This is why I am so annoyed and frustrated by much of the debate on immigration. It is absurd to hear statements like "immigrants don't want to assimilate," or "immigrants don't want to become part of America, learn English." On the contrary, when you are a recent immigrant, your love for America is possibly stronger than anybody else's. You chose to come to America. You are not here because your parents, grandparents, or great-grandparents preceded you. It is the classic immigrant story, true just as much for Cuban Americans, Mexican Americans, Salvadoran Americans, as it was for Irish, Germans, Italians or any of the many other immigrant groups that have helped build this country. You choose America, you choose to leave your home because something went wrong. This country opens its arms to you, and you want to fight for your country. This is your country now; you belong to it, it belongs to you, equally as much as it does to your neighbor. Those who argue to the contrary should perhaps take a trip like mine to Alabama and Texas. There is much they can learn from such an experience.

Over 60 percent of Miami's residents are foreign born. Our success can largely be attributed to this diversity. In fact, American cities with strong immigrant populations continue to outpace other cities in terms of economic growth. It is these cities that continue to serve as the economic engines of America. In my travels throughout the United States, I have been blessed with the opportunity to meet numerous immigrant families from all over the world. I have never heard any of them suggest that they want anything less than to be proud to be Americans, learning the English language, studying hard, and working to achieve the American Dream. And that's the way it should be for all first generation Americans.

My parents were no different. Sure, they always wanted me to retain Spanish, to not lose other aspects of my culture, but they very much wanted me to become an American: to speak English better than anyone else, to win the spelling bees. If you believe otherwise, you are suggesting that these immigrant parents do not want the best for their children or that they do not want them to succeed, because in America if you tell your child not to bother with learning English, with education, with any of that stuff, just stay in your enclave—then you're holding that child back. You're not pushing that child to take advantage of all the opportunities America offers. The notion of a parent taking that position is ludicrous.

There is no doubt that the process of assimilation can be tough. When we first arrived in Miami, we went to "El Refugio," the Cuban Refugee Center. The building, now called the Freedom Tower, is in public hands and has recently been designated a national historic landmark, two actions I led as mayor. It is Miami's version of Ellis Island. At the Center, we were given army rations that included huge blocks of cheese. Not individual, Kraft-sized American cheese slices: these were huge, bigger than a brick. We were also given powdered milk, powdered eggs, and Spam. To this day, many Cubans refuse to eat Spam because of the connotation that "this is what we had to eat." Of course, my mom, one of the greatest cooks in history, learned to make all kinds of dishes from Spam. It was our meat substitute. Instead of beef or pork chops, it was Spam. So we adjusted and were grateful that we had something to eat. By the way, I am one of the few who will still eat Spam.

When I was in second or third grade, my teacher, as part of the assimilation process, must have believed that every good American must like cottage cheese, celery, and biscuits. I could deal with the biscuits. The cottage cheese didn't taste like much to me. The celery: forget it. The Cuban diet doesn't include a lot of vegetables to begin with, let alone celery. The teacher, however, went around the class and instructed us to eat a stalk of celery. I refused. She grabbed the back of my head, stuck the celery stalk in my mouth, and said, "Bite!" So finally, I bit the crunchy stalk. I then ran to the bathroom and vomited. I was sent to the principal's office since, of course, I was not being cooperative. To this day, I will not eat celery. If you cut it in tiny pieces and put it in a tuna sandwich, I will find it. I have built in radar that goes off anytime I'm within five miles of it.

The process of assimilation should not include the stripping away of your customs and your culture. Rather, it should welcome them.

☐ ☐ ☐

CONCERNED ABOUT MY environment and my peers, my parents forced me to sit for an entrance exam at a private middle school: Belen Jesuit Prep School. The school, run by Jesuit priests, is the oldest Cuban school, having received its charter from Queen Isabella of Spain in 1854. It is Cuba's equivalent of Exeter or Choate. Belen is very well known in the Cuban community, and today is one of Miami's finest schools. Regrettably, one of our better-known graduates is Fidel Castro. Castro expelled the Jesuits from Cuba, causing them to relocate the school to a one classroom facility in downtown Miami.

I did my best to flunk the entrance exam.

Belen is an all-boy's school. I really didn't want to go to a school that did not have any girls—are you kidding me? Plus, there was the lure of the streets, and now they're going to send me where? To a school run by priests? All-boys, too? No way. Yet somehow I was admitted.

By the time I enrolled, the school had moved to an old ware-house that had, among other things, been used as a dance studio. It was also rumored that Al Capone stored wines and liquor at the warehouse during Prohibition. Three hundred students were enrolled from grades seven through twelve, in a building that had no windows. Today Belen is located in the western end of Miami-Dade County in facilities that resemble a small college campus. Not quite the physical structure it had in Cuba, an imposing, Pentagon-like structure, but an excellent facility nevertheless, with far more amenities than when I attended.

Today's students at Belen are obviously in a much better financial position than those who attended during my years. These students now include my children's generation. For one thing, my generation can afford to buy our children cars. When I was growing up, a giant group of us would try to squeeze into an old Volkswagen. Only a handful of us, at most, had parents who could afford a car. In fact, I used to go out on dates in a dairy and produce truck that a friend would use during the day to make deliveries.

While at Belen, at age fourteen, I landed my first job through CETA, the Comprehensive Employment Training Act. This was a program designed to provide jobs for youngsters from families at or below the poverty level. I remember the threshold was really high, but I met it. I earned $1.10 an hour, working as a janitor after school at Belen. Every day, I would start immediately after school to clean and do some of my assigned homework before practice (I had practice every day after school year-round since I was playing sports every season) or I would return to clean after practice. Throughout high school, I worked as a janitor, including weekends and in some cases during the summer as well. I also worked as a stock boy at the auto parts factory where my parents worked because the pay was a little better, helping the family out with the money I earned.

The student population at Belen was very small. Each grade was divided into an A class and a B class. I am not sure if it was by design, but during my six years at Belen, the A class seemed to perform better academically. Many of their parents came from a professional class. Many had been doctors or lawyers in Cuba. Although they too were struggling during those early years, they at least had a foundation that would serve them well in ultimately returning to financial success in America. As a result, their children had been exposed to more and often had more resources.

As you might expect, the B class housed the sports jocks, who also had a more rounded street education. I started out in seventh and eighth grades as part of the B class, which included a friend who had played baseball with me since we were kids. We both were still lured by the streets, being troublemakers and getting into fights. Going into ninth grade, my coach, Mariano Loret de Mola, one of my dad's oldest friends, took the two of us out of the B class and put us in the A class. I wasn't happy about the transfer since all my friends were in the B class. I really felt more at ease with the sports crowd than I did with the smart kids.

But an interesting thing happened when I went into the A class: peer competition. My athletic competitiveness was transferred to the classroom and I improved my grades dramatically. The coach knew that. That's why he pulled me out. Getting into Belen in the first place was a defining moment in my life; being transferred to the A group was another.

People ask me today how I keep my crazy schedule. It started at Belen. I would finish class, do my janitorial work either before or after practice, finish practice at 7:00 P.M., go home, shower, eat—somewhere in between visit my girlfriend—then, probably after 9:00 P.M. start my school work. At Belen you couldn't survive by simply cramming at the last minute. We had tests every week, several times a week. Basically, you were cramming every day. We would do our homework and projects as part of study groups. My classmates would come over to my house to study or I would go to their house. At midnight my parents, or their parents if I was at another student's house, would prepare café con leche so we could stay awake and study. That was my regular schedule then. And it continues today.

At Belen, it was assumed that you were going to college. There was no question about that; the only question was the career you would choose. But yes, you were going to college and you were going to be a professional, any profession.

My career path was also heavily influenced by my ninth-grade government teacher, Patrick Collins (who is still at Belen). On the first day of class, he gave us a challenge, "Ok, you guys are driving down some old country road in Alabama and a big sheriff comes over and arrests you because you look Hispanic or he just doesn't like you. What would you do? Do you know what your rights are?"

I wanted to know the answer, and it is at this the point that I began to focus on a legal career. There is also no doubt that my own personal experience of being uprooted from my country of birth, having a system fail because of the lack of the rule of law, and wondering how that was possible also played a significant role in my career decision. How can a country fail like this? Something must be structurally wrong with its institutions for that to happen. The pursuit of a legal career went hand in hand with a commitment to public service and social activism. The Jesuit education emphasizes the principles of always giving back; of remembering where you came from; and reaching out to help those who come after you, especially those less fortunate. That life should not be measured by the material riches one is able to secure, but rather by the value one adds to enhance the life of others. Our school's motto: Men for Others.

My classmates and I did well academically at Belen. There were forty students in our graduating class. I believe twelve would go on to become doctors. Another significant group would become lawyers, and many others succeeded in engineering, business, and other professions. We are all still friends. Sending me to Belen was one of the best things my parents ever did for me. I will forever be grateful for the sacrifices they made to make that possible.

Chapter 2 The Lost Generation Finds Its Way

TRAINED IN THE principle of Men for Others, I left high school with a strong sense of public service, wanting to help others. However, in order to do so, I would have to navigate uncharted waters. Politically and culturally, I was part of the first group of Cuban Americans who grew up in the United States. Even though we were born in Cuba, most of us were too young to remember much of anything. America is what we knew, but Cuba was never far away. Our parents and grandparents would never let us forget. One minute you're having dinner with your parents and the conversation revolves around Cuba and what is happening there. The next minute you're watching television shows in English, going to American movies, reading American books, attending an American school, listening to American music. You are exposed to all the influences of growing up in America, much like any other child your age. You're an American through and through.

This presented a huge challenge for those of us who grew up as members of the lost generation. I was raised in the 1960s and 1970s by a father who was very strict, very military, very old school. He even sported a crew cut. You don't know how difficult it was for him to come to the realization that just because I wanted to have long hair, wear shorts, jeans, or sandals didn't mean I was any less of a man. Culturally, in Cuba, men didn't wear sandals. Men also didn't wear shorts, especially if they were tight—that was a "gay" thing. Then there were tank tops or letting your hair grow long. Going to a dance at school wearing a tank top and stained jeans meant being stopped by my dad with the question, "What are you doing?"

There was this tremendous cultural clash between what my father was used to, how he was brought up, and this new reality in our new country. Thank God for my mom and my grandfather, who were both nearly always on my side: "It's just the way it is. That's how this country is. You have to understand," they would tell my dad. "You have to adapt." "No, I will never adapt" was his stern response.

Feeling comfortable in two often very different cultures created this same tension for most of my generation. We all went through much the same experience. A political gulf also separated my generation from that of my parents. Having been misled by a young charismatic leader into Communism, it was natural for them to think it could happen anywhere, including the United States. They were, understandably, more conservative, anti-communist and, because of the Bay of Pigs fiasco, anti-Kennedy, anti-Democratic Party. Cuba is where they were born, where they had started their lives. It didn't matter how long it took; they could not stop dreaming of their return. My generation shares these strong feelings about one day returning to live in or at least visit our country of birth. When we live the pain and witness the tears, those of us who have lost their parents no doubt reflect that their parents have passed away without realizing their dream of being buried in the country where they were born.

The political gulf between our generations widened when my call to public service led me to actively participate in a number of local organizations. Many in our community believed this action treasonous. Why are you forming or becoming a member of community-based organizations—groups dealing with the elderly, education and youth?

Because the plan was always to return to Cuba, there was no need for such organizations. It was as if being involved in any kind of organization not focused on overthrowing Castro was an acknowledgement of a truth no one wanted to admit—that we weren't going back, at least not for a very long time. This was a harsh reality for my parents and their generation. They were focused on change in Cuba. Many in my generation focused on change in Miami and of building our future in our new country.

□ □ □

I HAD MY first taste of politics in high school. It was in ninth grade, when I joined the A class, the class with the more studious kids. They were holding elections for class president. One of the students turned to me and asked if I would like him to nominate me. Another student offered to second the nomination. Fearing the smarter kids would not vote for a street jock, I accepted nevertheless and then became class president. It happened again in tenth and eleventh grades. My senior year, I was elected school president. This experience would serve as the launching pad for my career in public service.

At the first opportunity, I registered to vote as a member of the Democratic Party, despite the fact that my parents and most other Cuban Americans at the time were registering as Republicans. Friends of my parents would often refer to me as "Fidelito" (little Fidel) because of the Belen connection and because they considered me a liberal. "He's too young to be a communist, so we'll just call him a 'pinko' or 'little Fidel.'" Of course, they meant this endearingly.

The summer of my graduating year, I married my high school sweetheart. That was not my immediate post-graduation plan. Rather, I had planned to attend Columbia University in New York City on an academic scholarship, where I would join my best friend and former basketball teammate, Pedro Mencia. Concerned about starting a family so far from home, I decided to enroll at Miami Dade Community College, the largest community college in America, now known as Miami Dade College. I graduated with high honors at both Miami Dade College (1975) and Florida International University (1977). I attended both institutions on a full-time basis, worked full-time (often holding multiple jobs at one time), and regularly played the role of Mr. Mom, staying home to care for my son Manny while my wife worked and went to school to pursue her career in nursing.

Working full-time made it possible to pay for my studies and support my family. In fact, I never had to borrow money to finance any portion of my undergraduate education. Regrettably, while many state governments profess to lower taxes, they are continually raising fees, including college tuition. Tax and budgeting decisions are supposed to reflect a society's priorities. Obviously, these legislators do not place a high priority on postsecondary education and the future of our state. I am shocked by the costs of a college education today, and wonder whether it would have been possible for me to achieve what I did under these circumstances.

In juggling full-time work with a full-time school schedule, I was employed in a hodgepodge of jobs. I served as executive director of the Spanish Speaking Democratic Caucus. I served as a youth counselor and soccer coach for Hebraica (a social group of Cuban Jews); I had a field inventory route for the *National Enquirer*; I cleaned a bingo parlor between 4:00 and 7:00 A.M. (my first class started at 8:00 A.M.); I worked as an administrator of a surgical center at a local HMO; I was a private tutor in math and English for junior high and high school students; I served as campaign coordinator and chairman for various local and state races; and I would continue to do weekend and summer work at the auto parts factory where my parents still worked.

I attended the University of Miami School of Law. During my first year, I secured student loans (all of which were paid off on schedule). It was the policy of the law school to schedule classes throughout the day so that students would not be able to hold an outside job during their first year. After my first year, I was fortunate to secure a clerking job at an old-line Miami law firm, and I continued thereafter to work full-time throughout the balance of law school, while maintaining a full class load. I became the first member of my family to be awarded a college and professional degree.

☐ ☐ ☐

ALTHOUGH I WAS quite busy studying, working, and raising a family, I never lost sight of politics. My first foray occurred immediately after graduating from high school. In 1973, I worked on my first political campaign. The mayor of Miami, David Kennedy, had been removed from office. Maurice Ferre had been appointed to fill out the remainder of Kennedy's term and was now standing for election. A local business-man, Jim Angleton, was running against Ferre and against public corruption. It was music to the ears of a young idealist.

One Saturday morning, I drove to Overtown, a black neighborhood of Miami. The Ministers-Laymen Group in Overtown hosted a weekly breakfast and that day they were staging a debate between the mayoral candidates. I had already pegged Ferre as part of the same corrupt politics that had spawned Kennedy. Angleton portrayed himself as a religiously motivated businessman who wanted to change the world, change Miami. I thought to myself: that's just what Miami needs, someone like him.

I approached him after the debate and offered to help in his campaign. And I did. This was to be my first actual campaign job. We had an incredible grassroots operation, which included many of my Belen friends whom I recruited. With a throng of young volunteers, we walked door-to-door throughout the city. We did well, but Angleton fell a few points short. Nearly thirty years later I ran for mayor against Maurice and beat him.

I soon became deeply involved in Democratic Party politics. I became executive director of the Spanish Speaking Democratic Caucus. I was the kid in a group of very prominent community leaders. At Miami Dade College, I helped form a Young Democrats chapter that became the largest in the State of Florida and helped elect a statewide president from Miami, Kendall Coffey, who coincidentally would become my law partner years later.

I continued to sharpen my organizational skills within the Democratic Party. In 1974, the local party was controlled by Joe Robbie, former owner of the Miami Dolphins. Robbie had come to Miami from Minnesota, where he had been a state house member. He also had connections with Hubert Humphrey, the Minnesota senator and former vice president. The local executive committee—of which Robbie was chairman—comprised forty men and forty women. A group of young organizers—Mike Abrams, Sergio Bendixen, Mike O'Donovan, and myself (just to name a few)—believed it was time for a change in the local party structure. Joe Robbie did not represent our generation. We organized our own slate of eighty candidates to run for the executive committee. We called it Campaign 74. Our slate won and we elected Mike Abrams chair of the local party. We then took our "machine" statewide, electing Alfredo Duran, a member of the Spanish Speaking Democratic Caucus, chair of the Florida Democratic Party. Then we helped elect Jimmy Carter president of the United States.

In January 1975, I attended a college Young Democrats convention in Atlanta. Carter had just announced his candidacy, and was considered a long shot. Jimmy Who? At the gala dinner, the speakers were Andrew Young, Julian Bond, Maynard Jackson, . . . and Jimmy Carter. The first three wowed the group. The Watergate scandal (which had led to the resignation of President Richard M. Nixon) was still very much the rallying cry for young idealists. They were all very funny and very articulate. After the dinner, almost everyone ran to Young, Bond, and Jackson. Everyone wanted to meet them, secure their autographs, and get pictures with them. Jimmy Carter was standing by himself, in a corner of the room.

I have always cheered for the underdog. Feeling sorry to see him standing by himself, I decided to approach him and introduce myself. After a brief conversation, he invited me to join him for a cup of coffee. It was just the two of us; we spoke for hours. Mostly, I just listened to the reasons he had for running for president, and to the multiple references to his honesty (post-Watergate). On the drive back to Miami, I reflected on our conversation. He's a decent man, a good man; he has a pretty progressive record. As soon as I returned, I contacted Alfredo, Mike, and Sergio with an idea.

At the time, many of us were highly concerned about George Wallace, the white segregationist governor of Alabama who had run for the presidency in 1972 and performed better than expected—even outside the South. Democrats worried that Wallace might perform even better than he had in 1972, possibly winning the primaries in states like Michigan and Illinois. He had to be stopped early and his campaign had to be derailed in the South. If Wallace were to pick up momentum in the Southern primaries, who knew what could happen in the later primary states? And, in the South, where's the best place to beat him? Florida. But how do we beat him in Florida? The answer for me was Jimmy Carter, another Southern governor who could win Florida. He's progressive enough to appeal to the more progressive side of the party, but he's still a Southern governor and can connect with the Southern Democratic conservatives. Carter had the right combination. The group agreed to support his candidacy.

We started a statewide organization for him and held the first mock convention vote by the Florida Democratic Party—a straw vote that proved to be instrumental to his candidacy. The straw vote was a great way to bring exposure to your candidate (the same strategy would later work well for another Southern governor, Bill Clinton). The party faithful and leaders vote, and the candidate the national pundits never expected would win, does. That is what we did for Carter. The headlines went from "Jimmy Who?" to "Carter Wins Florida Straw Vote."

The strategy and execution were a testament to our ability to organize and mobilize a strong turnout at the convention. Although it is never simply one factor that determines winning or losing an election, there can be no doubt that winning the straw vote gave Carter a huge lift, attracting the support necessary for him to later win the Florida primary, and ultimately win the presidency. Interestingly, a Carter presidency was not my original plan. In fact, after Florida, he was no longer my candidate. I merely wanted to beat Wallace and open the field for other candidates I was more prone to support for the presidency.

During my early years, I also devoted a significant amount of time helping get Cuban Americans elected into office at all levels of government. Those first campaigns were extremely tough. It was practically impossible for a Diaz to beat a Smith, regardless of qualifications. Voting patterns essentially followed demographic lines. Electing the first Cuban American judges required first convincing our Florida governors to fill vacancies with Cuban Americans. Governor Bob Graham (later U.S. senator) is to be commended for heeding our call to make these early appointments. However, once appointed, our attention turned to helping them get elected. I was actively involved in both efforts, lobbying our governors to appoint Cuban Americans and helping the appointees and non-incumbents organize their judicial campaigns.

The electoral process was itself a game, even before qualifying to run. The game was to succeed in running unopposed. For the most part, only a handful of people actually ran for judicial office. There were plenty of seats and only a few candidates. Naturally, Cuban American candidates would be vulnerable in any race with even a handful of candidates.

Here is an illustration of the game. In order to protect the few Cuban American incumbents and candidates, I was required to meet with a political operative who for years had been the behind-the-scenes kingpin of judicial campaigns. He singlehandedly decided which candidates run for which seats. He would threaten me with running his candidate(s) against one of the Cuban Americans. Of course, if we retained his services, our candidate stood a much better chance of running unopposed. Committed to breaking down this long-standing, albeit pathetic practice, our candidates refused to pay his fees and instead relied on me to play poker with the operative. Since he represented candidates running for other offices, I would match his threat with an equal threat, that we would rally the Cuban American community in opposition to his other candidates. Of course, this was a complete bluff; I had no such power. I don't believe anyone has that power.

But, we had to play the game. The final test of our efforts would occur on the last day of qualifying. At this point, candidates wishing to qualify would have to appear physically in Tallahassee, our state capital, and file their papers by noon. The game went down to the wire as the operatives and potential candidates walked the halls at the very last minute, trying to determine whom to run against. I would stand outside the secretary of state's office all morning, waiting and watching to see which candidates were running for judge. Rumors were rampant, and in the end we learned how the game was played and how to win. I am so proud of that early group of Cuban American judges and candidates— Mario Goderich, Maria Korvick, Gisella Cardonne Dienstag, Margarita Esquiroz, and others. They served or continue to serve us with great distinction and in the process refused to be threatened by the old political system and stood on their principles. And in so doing, they virtually eliminated the game and paved the way for many others who followed them onto the bench. Being adequately represented in the judiciary by reflecting the community it represents is absolutely critical in ensuring a fair and just society.

While fighting for Cuban American judicial candidates, I also turned my attention to the Florida Legislature and the creation of single-member districts: districts where people elect only one person to represent them in a legislative body. Our success in this area helped not only Cuban Americans, but African Americans as well.

The Florida Legislature was dominated by white males. The system of multimember districts had made it impossible for Cuban Americans and other minorities to win a legislative seat. There simply were not enough pockets of minority voters located within these large districts. Single-member districts were the only plausible solution to achieve minority representation in the legislature. Again, I spent a significant amount of time lobbying in Tallahassee. Ironically, I met a considerable amount of resistance from my own local delegation made up almost exclusively of Democrats. I was well aware of the fact that one of the by-products of single-member districts would likely be the election of Cuban American Republicans—which is in fact what later happened. Nevertheless, this issue was about principle; from a policy point of view, single-member districts are essential to achieve diversity in Tallahassee. This was my priority. Separately, it would be up to the Democrats and Republicans to elect their candidates. But that should not detract from the goal.

We succeeded in persuading the legislature to adopt single-member districts. This could not have happened without the leadership of the Senate president, a conservative Southern Democrat from the Florida panhandle, Dempsey Barron. After spending a considerable amount of time with him, I became convinced that he truly believed in our goals and that he very much wanted this legislation to serve as his legacy for Florida. He was willing to overlook plenty, both personally and politically. Yet even when some of my Democratic friends from South Florida tried to circumvent the process, he would call them on the carpet in front of me and admonish them in his deep Southern drawl, "Heard y'all are tryin' to do this. That's not gonna happen."

After the legislation passed in 1982, we elected our first Cuban Americans to the Florida Legislature, Ileana Ros Lehtinen (now in Congress), Humberto Cortina, and Lincoln Diaz Balart (recently retired from Congress). Equally as important to me, we also saw the election of Carrie Meek, the first African American since Reconstruction to become a member of the Florida Senate and later the U.S. House of Representatives (her son, Kendrick, later occupied her seat and unsuccessfully ran for the U.S. Senate). The Florida Legislature today is much more reflective of Florida's diverse population. This was made possible by the passage of the legislation creating single-member districts. In fact, Florida was one of the few, if not the only, state to adopt single-member districts voluntarily and without litigation.

□ □ □

MY BACKGROUND IN electoral politics, especially my love for statistical analysis of voting results and patterns, propelled me in yet another direction politically. My multiple campaign experiences often involved polling. In 1984, I visited friends at the Spanish International Network, now known as Univision, and offered to do exit polling for the station. They were not familiar with exit polling. In those days, very few people were, including the English language networks in Miami.

The station management agreed. The network had no budget for exit polling or me. This effort was to be strictly experimental, and, in fact, they were taking a huge gamble because I was a friend and they knew that I had organized many campaigns that involved polling. We had no resources whatsoever. I had such a skeleton crew that even I had to stand at a polling place several times during the day in order to make sure I had enough of a statistical sample. I would then drive back to my office and use a calculator with a huge spreadsheet—I don't mean Excel, but the old ledger spreadsheet—to run the numbers. Finally, I would rush to the station, finalize the results, and prepare for live TV.

My job was to announce the results live at 7:00 P.M., immediately after the polls had closed. It was just minutes before going on the air, and I still didn't have the final results. My team was scrambling, trying to finalize the data I had provided them. The anchors were on the set, ready to start the newscast. The station had announced throughout that day I would be introducing this new methodology that would allow the station to announce the day's winners even before the first votes were counted. Viewers would no longer have to stay up late into the evening to find out if the candidates of their choice won or lost.

I asked the anchors to stall for as long as possible. We were almost ready. As we go live, the anchors begin to talk, and talk, and talk. It was a long introduction. Finally, a member of my team literally crawls on the floor over to me with the final numbers. The anchors see this and say, "Let's turn it over to Manny Diaz." I pull the papers from his hands, turn to the camera, and say, "Today's election results are . . . ."

This was the first time exit polling had been done in Miami, and I continued to announce winners and losers at 7:00 P.M. every election night in the years to come. Of course, this newly introduced political methodology had plenty of skeptics. Every election night, history repeated itself. A television news crew would be assigned to each candidate on election night. The candidate I projected to lose would reject the projection, instead suggesting that we needed to wait until all the ballots were counted. His or her precinct results had not yet been counted. Even today, many candidates are in denial, but the process works.

Continuing to employ my love for statistics, I then devoted a significant amount of time and effort in determining which municipality in Miami-Dade County had the best and earliest possibility of electing our first Cuban American mayor. Much to the surprise of many, I concluded that a small, one-precinct town in Miami-Dade County called Sweetwater was beginning to show an increase in Hispanic voter registration and that this would be our best shot at getting our first Cuban American elected as mayor. We understood it was going to be a real uphill battle, but nonetheless we all decided to get behind the candidacy of José Montiel. We raised money, walked door-to-door, fully knowing we would not win this time, but we created an awareness in Sweetwater that ultimately did lead to the election of our first Cuban American mayor. We broke the ice. Sometimes you have to lose to win.

My experience with exit polling, and the multiple statistical studies and analysis I had performed throughout the years, allowed me to become very familiar with practically all precincts in the City of Miami. Not only had I grown up in these precincts, I had studied them, walking door to door while campaigning for other candidates. This grassroots experience served me very well in my own mayoral campaign.

Chapter 3 Creating My Own Politics

NUMEROUS INDIVIDUALS INSPIRED me to enter public service while I was growing up. If we are going to change politics in this country, we have an obligation to inspire and encourage today's young people to heed the call for public service, advocate for their vision of their future, and run for public office. This is how I got started, and this is what we must do for them.

I first began by managing typical low budget campaigns that instilled in me a love for grassroots organizing. These campaigns allow you the opportunity to meet your neighbors, the voters you seek to represent. You learn so much from listening to what people have to say instead of relying on a pollster. This way, your message is formed by people who will share with you their dreams and concerns. Unfortunately, politics in America today has become all about money, paid media, and politicians imposing their ideas on voters.

Michael O'Donovan was a dear friend who passed away at a very young age. We had met during the Angleton for Mayor campaign in the City of Miami and later worked together on Campaign '74. O'Donovan was very much like Bobby Kennedy, filled with charisma and passion. I ran his campaign for the State House of Representatives in 1976. Mike was running in a multimember district that was about the size of Rhode Island. I again recruited many of my former Belen classmates and developed a significant volunteer staff. Using an old school bus, thirty to forty of us would spread out through this enormous district. As a result, through our door-to-door efforts, we managed to visit a significant number of voters in the district—in many cases twice. We also ran phone banks. And we had only $5,000 in campaign funds to compete against a long-term incumbent. We failed to force a runoff by a mere 11 votes. It was devastating, but a great learning experience.

When I ran for mayor, many people thought that I would exclusively wage a media campaign. After all, I was known as a successful political fundraiser, a lawyer who would raise a lot of money. My opponents assumed I would lose because they had a political base of support and I did not, and you can't create or turn another's base quickly enough strictly through a media campaign. They forgot where I started, my political history. I had organized at the block level, the precinct level. I had walked many of these neighborhoods. I raised money and had a very good media campaign, but, more important, I also knocked on the front doors of 10,000 Miami homes. Another benefit of a grassroots campaign is that it is stealth—your opponents do not see you gaining on them. They can call the local media and inquire as to how much airtime I had bought for the week. They can watch my television ads in the comfort of their living rooms at home. They can convince themselves they know my campaign strategy. But, they cannot quantify the number of homes I have visited door-to-door. Occasionally, they may receive a call from a friend or supporter advising that I visited them at home, but there is absolutely no way for the candidate to know whether on that day, I visited only that house, 50, 100, or 200 houses.

My fundraising history began in 1985 while serving as general counsel for a Miami-based real estate company. In the mid-1980s, it was much easier to raise money for campaigns in Florida. The contribution limit was $3,000 per individual or corporation. We had a number of subsidiary and affiliated companies. Ten such companies could mean $30,000 in contributions. A candidate could visit our office and walk away with $30,000 in contributions without having to endure the typical campaign reception and customary stump speech.

Americans love political reforms. We believe that these reforms will somehow cleanse the political system. In most cases, however, they fail to achieve their intended purpose. Lowering fundraising limits has not reduced the amount of money in politics today; in fact, more money is raised and spent today than ever before. Members of Congress raise money full time and President Obama has targeted a billion dollars as a fundraising goal for his 2012 reelection campaign. I am a big believer in disclosure and transparency. As an individual, if you wish to contribute $10,000 to my campaign, I see no reason why you should not be allowed to. If you are a greedy, corrupt businessman who is apparently trying to curry favor with me, everyone will know. If a politician is taking $10,000 from a greedy, corrupt businessman, one can certainly choose not to vote for him or her. On the flip side, if limited to a $500 contribution, that same greedy, corrupt businessman will bundle checks totaling $10,000 from lawyers, accountants, doctors, friends, and family. And no one can really ever track the money with any degree of certainty.

In 1991, I started my law firm and continued to raise money for candidates, one of them being Bill Nelson, the current senator from Florida. During his 1994 campaign for state insurance commissioner (which he won), our firm was his largest fundraiser. Through Senator Nelson's campaign, we were able to connect with a statewide network of fundraisers in a state known as a significant source of campaign contributions for national candidates.

Campaigning and fundraising are an important part of my political history, but there is a third area that is just as important: becoming involved in local community-based organizations devoted to various important social issues. I served on the board of several of these organizations active in assisting members of the Cuban American community.

My participation in these organizations was driven not by political but by personal considerations. For example, I served as a member of the board of the Little Havana Activities and Nutrition Center. This organization is committed to Miami's elderly and now feeds over 20,000 seniors daily in its meals program. I joined the group because I saw that my grandparents were starting to age and had special needs. Thus, I recognized the importance of such programs for elderly Cuban Americans.

Now flash forward to my term as mayor. These same programs were substantially cut when President George W. Bush tried to eliminate Community Development Block Grant (CDBG) funding. A portion of the funding for these elderly feeding programs came from CDBG. Understand that for many of the seniors participating in these programs, this was their only hot meal of the day. In fact, most of them take some kind of bag with them and if they don't eat their two pieces of bread, they will take one home. They will have that piece of bread at night, with a café con leche. It's an essential and humane program.

When I funded my poverty initiative as mayor, I set aside a portion of these funds every year to fill the gap created by the federal cuts to CDBG. While we could not keep up with the increasing demand for this service, we could at least maintain the levels that existed before the cuts. Many politicians at the federal level will use seniors, children, and other groups as pawns in a greater political game, rarely understanding the effects of their decisions because, unlike a mayor, they don't have to look into the eyes of their constituents on a daily basis. Ironically, while running for office, every politician visits senior centers in search of votes, making promises they don't intend to keep. The seniors smile and often vote for these politicians, not realizing they are being used: very sad. Whereas Beltway dwellers can cut funding for these groups, I had to figure out how to replace the funds because the need is real and very much a part of life for many in Miami, just as it is in other cities in America.

I also served on the Board of Youth Co-Op, a local program targeted at Hispanic youth. As a product of CETA, I understood that with a push, you could provide someone like me the ability and the opportunity to get where I am today. Youth Co-op for me was about making sure that we continued to do that in Miami by providing summer jobs for Hispanic youth in poverty. Youth Co-op is still in operation, and it continues to grow. As mayor, I announced my first antipoverty program at Youth Co-op.

Of course, it should go without saying that part of my involvement with these groups was to make sure that there were opportunities for Cuban Americans in Miami, both from a political perspective and from a needs basis. At the time, ethnic divisions were apparent in Miami. Cuban Americans were a fairly substantial number in a city and county whose total population wasn't that large to begin with. Compare New York City, with eight million people; if 100,000 people become new residents, it doesn't have as large an impact as it does in a city like Miami with a population of just over 400,000. Obviously, there were going to be natural tensions with the white or Anglo community and with the African American community: immigrants are coming in, taking our jobs; "they don't speak our language," have storefront signs in Spanish, speak Spanish in elevators.

These tensions were brewing long before 1980. I thought that it was important for me to play a role in helping to ease them. I'm an American, raised here. I speak English. I'm on my way to law school. But at the same time, I am Cuban American and I understand what is happening in my community. I became involved with different ethnic and social community organizations throughout Miami, trying to understand what made us different, and more importantly what we shared in common.

⬚ ⬚ ⬚

WHEN I ENTERED law school in 1977, I did my best to curtail my political and community activities. My goal was to focus on law school, earn good grades, pass the bar exam, and start my profession.

"I don't want political jobs anymore," I thought. Then 1980, the year I graduated, would become one of the most difficult years in Miami's history. In the course of one year, Miami experienced the Mariel and Haitian boatlifts, and the Liberty City riots. We would become the riot capital of America. And then, in the midst of all this tension, a group in Miami used the referendum process to place an "Anti-Bilingual Ordinance" on the ballot. This was a first-of-its-kind "English-only" ordinance that would prohibit use of government funds to translate official documents.

Eduardo Padrón, now president of Miami Dade College, was chair of SALAD, the Spanish American League Against Discrimination. SALAD had been formed in 1974 as a civil rights advocacy organization for the Spanish American community in Miami. Padron asked me to serve as executive director of the organization. I was hesitant to accept his offer. My plan was to graduate, pass the bar, and begin practicing law. I certainly did not want this to be my first job out of law school. But with all that was going on, and knowing I could help close the divide between our different communities, I accepted Eduardo's plea. I became the chief spokesperson against the anti-bilingual ordinance, taking part in multiple debates and making numerous public and media appearances. Regrettably, the campaign became very bigoted. It became a legitimate way to expose the hatred people wanted to express. In the context of campaigning, people seem to find it much easier to say things they would not ordinarily dare say.

The ordinance essentially called for making English the county's official language. I am not sure this was necessary because (a) the county does not need an official language and (b) no one was suggesting another official language other than English. During the debates, the underlying intent of the proponents became increasingly clear.

"We don't think ballots should be in a language other than English."

But that is mandated by the Civil Rights Act, I would reply. The ordinance would not change that.

"Well, we don't think there should be bilingual education in schools."

That's mandated by federal law as well. The ordinance would not change that either.

"Well," they would continue, *"we don't think that people should—when I walk into a store, the clerk shouldn't be speaking Spanish to people next to him. People walking down streets or in elevators should speak only English. Signs in stores should only be in English."*

Of course, none of this would be affected by the ordinance. You cannot legislate customer service or against rudeness. But when I pointed this out to people, they would respond: *"I don't care. I want to send you people a message."*

In fact, the only government-related function affected by the ordinance was Miami-Dade's Office of Latin Affairs, a small office with a single staffer that received nominal funding (similar offices had been established for blacks and women). The ordinance itself, however, was a strong statement: "We've put up with you guys for twenty years, and we're sending you a clear public statement that we're not happy with you." With Mariel as a backdrop, this was a tipping point for many people.

In the early 1970s, Miami-Dade County had adopted a resolution declaring the county bilingual and bicultural. This made sense. County leaders realized the potential long-term economic benefit to Miami as a gateway to the Americas and the potential investments that would result from that. It was just a resolution, not an ordinance. In 1980 one of the concerns voiced was that this resolution should be repealed. But the ordinance would also not repeal this resolution. It was pretty ugly. People were saying nasty things, and it was very divisive in the community. The woman who led the anti-bilingual effort under the banner of Citizens for Dade United, Emmy Shaffer, was herself of Eastern European descent, with a very strong accent.

So there I was, a recent law school graduate; a young man, nicely dressed, with no discernible accent. It was so upsetting to often hear, *"Well, this is not about you. You're acceptable. It's about all those other guys. You are not like the rest of them.*" During one of my televised debates with Emmy, she leaned over during a commercial break and told me, "I want you to meet my granddaughter." She was trying to set me up with her granddaughter! On one hand, I had horns on my head. On the other, she wanted to introduce me to her granddaughter? I could not help but laugh.

We were polling 75 to 25 percent against us, and in the end, we only lost 60 to 40 percent. The ordinance was repealed in 1993, however, and the issue has never come up again. I did an analysis of the voting patterns, and found that many of my civil rights colleagues actually voted against us. If you looked at areas with predominantly black residents and those with heavy concentrations of Jewish voters, it showed that they actually sided with Emmy Shaffer. The reasoning behind that vote was interesting. The main conflict with the black community was always about how Cubans had come in and "taken our jobs." The Jewish community had a different reason. What I heard, not so much from the younger as from the older generation, was: when my parents and grandparents came to America, they were attacked and ridiculed because they spoke a different language. If that happened to them or me, then it should happen to you.

Of course, that line of reasoning makes no sense. We have become a little more progressive and enlightened in America. Your parents and grandparents went through what they went through. We can't change that. However, why should we wish that others experience the same pain brought about by intolerance? Or so I tried to argue. In rebuttal, I would hear, "No, no, we couldn't put up our signs in our language, and we were ridiculed and others would shame us into becoming Americans and speaking English and forgetting our traditions and language and our culture, and that should apply to you." I would expect to hear this in areas like south Miami-Dade, a very rural area during that time and predominantly white. I expected that group to support the ordinance, but it was very disappointing for me to see people I had stood with on so many other issues standing against me on this one.

Of course, the ordinance changed nothing. Everybody yelled at one another for a few months and simply drifted farther apart. With the ordinance's passage, a legislator in Tallahassee tried to do the same thing at a state level, which we were able to defeat every time he tried. He finally gave up. Then a similar measure was introduced in Congress. We took our fight to D.C. and helped kill it there as well. In the end, it only achieved a meaningless victory in Miami-Dade County.

After the anti-bilingual ordinance referendum vote, I stepped down as executive director of SALAD, started my law practice, and became a member of the SALAD board (I later became vice chairman and chairman—one of only six in SALAD's 26-year history). It was as a board member that I worked against similar bills in Tallahassee and Washington. In fact, a significant part of my work with SALAD involved fighting one of those bills, the Immigration Reform and Control Act of 1986 (the Simpson-Mazzoli Act), in the U.S. Congress.

Simpson-Mazzoli was an anti-immigrant bill, targeted against Latinos, and, as originally conceived, very regressive. I positioned SALAD to join with other Hispanic organizations, such as the National Council of La Raza. We were always isolated in Miami and many Mexican American and Puerto Rican organizations didn't consider us part of the national Hispanic coalition. I helped change that. Through the Spanish International Network/Univision, we held a series of retreats with Hispanic leaders from around the country, including former HUD Secretary Henry Cisneros, members of Congress, and others from the Hispanic national business community. We would meet regularly to discuss a national Hispanic agenda. Simpson-Mazzoli was at the top.

There were issues involving federal ID cards, undocumented workers and penalties, and due process rights. What was important for us was making it clear that, even though we are all Latinos, we are from different countries and have different issues that are important to us.

For example, the issue of crossing borders and ID cards does not affect Cuban Americans as much as it does Mexican Americans. Frankly, it's not part of our daily lives. But for us, the 1966 Cuban Adjustment Act, modeled after the Hungarian Adjustment Act, is a path for all of us to achieve citizenship. Under the Cuban Adjustment Act, a Cuban who could get into the United States could become a permanent resident in a year. Five years later such individuals could apply for citizenship. It was a really short-circuit approach to becoming a citizen, one made available to Cubans because if you're fleeing a Communist-run state, you're assumed entitled to political asylum.

Simpson-Mazzoli called for the repeal of the Cuban Adjustment Act. Naturally, most other advocacy groups in the country were not averse to repealing it: Why should Cubans and no one else have this special right? I had to convince my new partners: "Don't touch it." That's important to us. I understand we are in an exclusive club, but the way to fix that is not to eliminate it. Instead, I will support your priorities, and if there are others who should also receive this special right, let's join forces to advocate for them. In fact, I lobbied extensively for an adjustment act for Haitians. Some people in the Cuban American community were critical of my efforts, asking why I should care so much about the rights of other immigrants, including Haitians. My response was two-fold. First, they deserve it. They are here; they have been going through conditions similar to the ones we experienced; they are Caribbean and, like us, they need the opportunity. But let's be practical too: we have the Cuban Adjustment Act. And the best thing we can do to keep attention away from the Act is to work on making sure that this deserving group benefits from a similar law.

The Cuban Adjustment Act was not repealed under Simpson-Mazzoli; it was saved and remains until this day, albeit altered to some degree with the "wetfoot/dryfoot" distinction that came into play many years later during the Clinton administration—a policy that grew out of concern over how to deal with a dramatic increase in Haitian refugees setting sail and landing in Florida. Many Haitians were being detained at sea and sent back to Haiti as the administration struggled with how to deal with this influx. And, of course, it all came back to the treatment Cubans receive. If they're Cuban, we don't send them back, the thinking went; in fact, we have a little party for them on the Coast Guard cutter before we bring them into America. That is unfair. They're not being treated the same.

So this really bad policy was created. Now, if you are able to touch American soil, you can stay. If we stop you at sea, we will send you back. The implementation of the policy created images few of us can forget: Cubans jumping off dinghies and inner tubes in the ocean, trying to swim the last half mile to get onshore, and Coast Guard cutters, with large fire hoses, hosing them down, while Coast Guard officials jumped in the water to chase them before they could reach the shore. It was and continues to be an absurd policy. But it remains the law of the land. Simpson-Mazzoli itself was passed in 1986—a version of it, but not the more draconian version that had originally been submitted.

◻ ◻ ◻

I WANT TO return for a moment to 1980 and elaborate some more on the Mariel boatlift. This was a unique moment in Miami's history. The backlash was very strong against Cuban Americans, as evidenced by the anti-bilingual ordinance. The Cuban experience had always been portrayed as a Horatio Alger story. This group had been popularly described as people who came to the United States with a dime in their pocket, unable to speak English, and yet, within twenty years, had accomplished much. Indeed, by 1980 that was the case. Some Cubans already held public office. Businesses had been started and prospered. Cubans had progressed at a faster pace than any other immigrant group in American history.

Between April and October 1980, however, Florida was inundated with a surge of more than 100,000 Cubans. We all know the story now. Fidel Castro said he would allow Cubans to emigrate to the United States from Mariel Harbor. However, he attached conditions: you can take your fifteen relatives with you, but you also have to take these five other men I have just pulled out of prisons or mental hospitals. And when I say "prison," I don't mean he was expelling prisoners of conscience: I mean pretty bad guys.

All of a sudden, Miami was awash in bad guys who grew up in a system where there aren't many options and you depend on the government for everything, or you do whatever is necessary, including a life of crime, in order to survive. Unwillingly, this group were sent to Miami, no longer able to depend on anyone; now they're on their own. They were told, "If you go to school and work hard, the American Dream is possible." But many of these former prisoners had no interest in achieving the American Dream. They grew up knowing only a life of crime and wished to continue that life. During the early 1980s, the homicide rate in Miami shattered all previous records. Miami became known as the murder capital of the United States. We would also become the riot capital and drug capital of America, with the influx of cocaine cowboys and police corruption. Those were very tough times.

Mariel severely hurt the image of Cuban Americans. Suddenly, at a national level, the perception of Cubans shifted from Horatio Alger to a bunch of thugs. But as with most ten-second sound bites, the debate centered not around the bad guys but on Mariel itself as a bad thing. Good people were viewed through the lens of a few bad ones. Even in the Cuban community there was a negative reaction to this influx of new Cubans. "We don't want those people" was the common response. Bucking this popular trend, I argued the opposite, trying to convince others that these individuals were also Cubans. Yes, there were some troubling elements among them. These bad guys should go to jail. If they commit a crime they should be deported. But they were also entitled to the same legal protections we all enjoy. No matter how distasteful that may have seemed to a few, you can only protect your rights by protecting the rights of others. I urged caution not to overreact to the times; to deal with the issue under our system of laws and not allow our own response to be dictated by the unfortunate negative publicity.

Some people did. For example, Joe Davis, Miami-Dade County medical examiner, described "these people" as "animals" or words to that effect. Many of us protested against this characterization, and he was ultimately forced to resign. Of course, others joined the chorus. It became popular for Miamians to drive around with bumper stickers that read "Will the last American to leave please bring the Flag." Emotions ran very high.

It bears repeating that this was exactly the result Castro envisioned when he forced Cuban Americans to add these unwanted passengers to their boats. One must remember his public relations nightmare, having announced that Cubans on the island who wanted to leave were free to do so. Ten thousand Cubans responded by storming the Peruvian Embassy in Havana, seeking asylum and safe passage out of Cuba. If the Cuban people were so happy with his regime, why did so many want to leave? Given the opportunity, how many more would choose to leave? His response was to force Cuban Americans who had traveled to Cuba to pick up relatives to load their boats with hardened criminals and patients from mental institutions. In so doing, he turned public opinion against those Cubans truly in search of freedom and their relatives in Miami.

A large number of the criminals settled in what is today known as South Beach. Believe it or not, during those years it was actually cheaper to live there than in most other places in Miami. Everyone now associates South Beach with glitz and glamor, but in 1980 I opened a political campaign headquarters there and couldn't convince any volunteers to work in that office. South Beach was dangerous, extremely dangerous.

The federal government left it to us in Miami to deal with this problem. We tried telling those who would listen that most of the new arrivals had relatives in the area, and that they would assimilate. It was only a matter of time. Absorbing this large influx would have been nearly seamless, if it were not for the criminal element. Again, the vast majority of those who arrived came not with the idea of becoming a ward of the state, but with a desire to find a job right away, secure a driver's license immediately, and move out of relatives' homes and apartments into their own places as soon as possible. Thirty years later, we know that this is exactly what happened; the good guys assimilated and, like those who came before them, have made significant contributions in all areas of life.

Nationally, however, the perception lingered. An early Gallup poll asked: Who would you least like to have as a neighbor? The number one answer was a member of a cult (remember, we were only a couple years past the mass suicide of followers of Jim Jones in Guyana). Second? Cubans. Incredible! It was difficult to understand how a sixty-five-year-old woman living in Iowa would say, "I don't want a Cuban living next to me." She may not have ever met a Cuban or even locate Cuba on a map, but she feared us enough not to want to live next door to us! An image, a perception, had been created that needed to be combated. We took a real beating.

Then there was *Scarface*.

Hollywood jumped on the bandwagon and remade this famous classic, except now Cubans were the gangsters. The film was released in 1983, and a city commissioner at the time wanted to block filming in Miami, saying the city would not issue any film permits. This was ridiculous. It not only infringed on free speech, but played into the stereotype of Cubans as intolerant. It made us look bad. Again I was on the "nonpopular" side of the issue. I figured that the movie was going to be made anyway, with or without input from Cuban Americans, so I thought that it would be best to try to influence the outcome. Movies create jobs and the production also spends a lot of money. The cast and crew may go to a Cuban-owned dry cleaning business or eat at a Cuban restaurant.

In the end, *Scarface* was not filmed in Miami. I picked up the phone and called the president of Universal Studios. After talking to him, we were able to get a few scenes filmed in the city, but most scenes were shot in California. We also managed to have some impact on the movie. By reaching out to the executive producer, I was allowed to read the script and provide comment.

I could not deny that bad people had been among those who arrived with the Mariel boatlift. In the movie, Al Pacino played one of them. However, it was equally important to show that most were decent, hardworking people. We were able to incorporate dialogue in the movie that reflected this. The mother of Al Pacino's character refuses to take his drug money, saying it's dirty cash, Cubans don't do that; we earn our money the right way. There was Cuban American law enforcement presenting a contrast to Al Pacino's character, Tony Montana. This was the same sort of controversy that surrounded *The Godfather* and the Italian community in the United States. Don Corleone was not every Italian, Tony Montana was not every Cuban. That conclusion comes from conversation rather than isolation. This way, perhaps the woman in Iowa will not believe Tony Montana represents every Cuban.

In this same way, the perception was created that Cubans politically only care about one issue—toppling Castro. This perception was perpetuated by politicians who would try to outdo themselves on how anti-Fidel they could be. Those in my generation had to change this. I was perhaps the first Cuban American to run for office not based on how anti-Fidel I was. Before me, a Cuban American's position on Fidel was always part of his or her platform: "I am more anti-communist, more anti-Fidel than my opponent, so vote for me." That was a central element in campaigns. In my case, I always told people that I have my own personal beliefs, and obviously I despise Fidel just as much as everyone else does. But, if I'm elected mayor of Miami, I'm elected to represent all the people of Miami. I'm not elected to advocate for a particular foreign policy. If people want to know my personal opinion on issues I'll be happy to share it, but my personal, strong feelings about Fidel Castro have nothing to do with my job as mayor.

Many politicians in Miami were on Spanish-language media pounding on Castro and communism because they believed Cuban Americans couldn't get enough of such rhetoric. I broke that mold. I was elected without mentioning the "F word." I served for eight years without mentioning the F word. I was elected and governed to improve education, to create prosperity and jobs, to fight to reduce crime, to reclaim our parks—issues that should be the focus of any mayor. And it is on this basis that every voter should determine whether to vote for me. Yet, it was because of Castro, and my country's response to him, that I ran for office. It involved another six-year-old Cuban boy: Elián González.

THE ELIÁN GONZÁLEZ story begins on Thanksgiving Day in 1999, a month after my dad had passed away. Fishermen found six-year-old Elián holding onto an inner tube off the coast of Fort Lauderdale, Florida. His mother, Elizabeth Broton, and several others had drowned after the small boat they were on capsized two days earlier. A court granted legal custody of Elián to his great-uncle Lázaro González and his family in Miami. We didn't realize it at the time, but the stage was being set for something much larger than finding a home for a motherless child.

Early on, U.S. attorney general Janet Reno seemed to indicate that this was a simple immigration matter that did not merit high-level involvement from Washington. Castro soon decided he wanted the boy back. The U.S. Mission in Havana received a communiqué from the Cuban government asking that the boy be returned. As I mentioned earlier in this book, children in Cuba are considered wards of the state, so in that view, the action was reclaiming someone that belonged to Cuba. Elián's father, Juan Miguel González, was summoned to Havana. Fidel put his arm around him, sending the message, "You're mine." Fidel was now in control.

Then the Cuban American National Foundation, an influential lobbying group, became involved. They ratcheted up their advocacy, distributing posters and flyers in support of Elián staying in the United States to grow up in freedom.

The González family in Miami advised us that Juan Miguel was aware that Elián was coming to the United States. He was aware that Elián's mother was leaving with him. He had asked his aunt in the United States, Caridad González, to get visas for him, his wife, and their new child. Juan Miguel had sold an old car to get money to pay for him and his family to leave. In fact, the extended González family was very close. In the months before Elián's crossing, members of the entire family had been in Cuba, where everyone had taken part in a pig roast in celebration of their visit. This was not an estranged family. This was not a family that was in dispute and fighting. This was a very close-knit family. Castro and politics tore them apart.

From that point on, this matter took on a life of its own. What had been to that point a routine matter now became an international political tug-o-war. The case started to move its way into the court system, both at the state and federal levels. The state court had already granted custody of Elián to his Miami family, but it would ultimately be the federal court process that received worldwide attention.

In January 2000, my law firm received a call on behalf of Elián's family in Miami. My partner, Kendall Coffey, took the call. A former U.S. Attorney for the Southern District of Florida, Kendall is an outstanding litigator, one of the best I have ever met. The case was becoming more complex, now involving difficult federal issues including significant Constitutional questions. Even before we received the call, most of us in the office had been closely following the case and wondering what we would do differently if we were representing the parties. Now we would get that chance.

Kendall approached me and our other partner, Juan O'Naghten, "We have just been asked to represent Elián and his family. What do you guys think?" Obviously, we first had to consider the question from a business perspective. Once you commit to a case of this magnitude, the fiscal impact on the practice is going to be very substantial. A case like this can become—and became, in fact—very, very time consuming. We devoted six months, half a year, of our practice to Elián's case pro bono. The entire firm wasn't involved—we tried to keep a lot of the associates working on generating income so we could pay the rent, but certainly the principals were almost exclusively working on the case.

There was another, more personal, consideration for me.

I wanted to make sure of two things. I wanted assurances that if we accepted the engagement, we would captain the ship. In consultation with our client, we would make the calls, we would make the decisions. We would never accept (and would immediately resign in the face of) any effort to have our actions dictated by a committee, especially if other political agendas were involved. This was to be handled no differently from any of our other cases. I also had to be convinced that the case was not a pretense for someone's political agenda. I needed to know if the family truly wanted that which was in the best interest of Elián and to honor the wish of his late mother, who paid the ultimate price to secure Elián 's freedom.

I met with Elián 's two great uncles, Lázaro and Delfín González. I would also meet Caridad González, their sister, and Marisleysis González, Lázaro's daughter and Elián's cousin. They shared their family history, one that was remarkably similar to mine. I felt a connection to them. This reassured me that they were indeed genuine and looking out for Elián. I advised Lázaro and Delfín that, as their attorneys, it was essential that we be in charge of the matter; that they place their trust in us and follow our advice. One quick bit of advice: we asked that they immediately replace the Cuban flags outside their house with American flags. They agreed.

So we got past these issues. I then sat there for an additional hour or two just to look into their eyes, to get a true sense of their motivation. I came away convinced that their motives were real. There was no political agenda on their part; this was just a family matter, and should have stayed as such. But politicians could not resist getting involved. Having experienced firsthand the hurt of family separation, I understood the family completely. When I was six years old, my mom also left my father behind in Cuba and came to the United States so that I could grow up in freedom. The difference was that my mom survived and Elián's did not. This case became very personal.

We accepted—we would represent the family.

In the six months that followed, the case worked itself all the way up to the U.S. Supreme Court. What many people have yet to realize is that the merits and substance of the case were never heard. The real issue—whether it is in the best interest of Elián for his father or his family in Miami to have custody—never went before a judge. Instead, we spent months debating a strictly procedural issue: whether or not he would ever get a day in court to then have the real issue determined. For reasons yet unknown, Washington's attitude changed dramatically. The government would devote an amazing amount of resources to this case, directing the full brunt of the Justice Department against only a handful of Miami attorneys working pro bono on a routine immigration matter. Elián never got his day in court.

Why was the government so interested in denying this one six-year-old child his day in court? This question continues to perplex us. We have an extensive body of law in this country to determine the best interests of a child with regard to custody. The fact is that at this very moment, judges are determining whether a father is fit, a mother is fit, whether grandparents are fit, to be a child's custodians. That happens every day in American courtrooms. This is what we wanted: to present the evidence as to why it was in Elián's best interest to stay with his family in the United States, and have a judge make a determination on that issue. Ultimately, the courts determined on procedural grounds—that included assorted immigration issues—that Attorney General Reno had complete and absolute discretion. If she felt Elián should not have a day in court, he shouldn't.

Reno and her lawyers began to engage in tactics to demoralize and wear us down. There were times at night when we were afraid to leave the office. Often, late into the evening, government lawyers would send a fax with some kind of threat or demand requiring a response from us by a certain time, usually early the following morning, or else. As the family's lawyers we would receive the fax, drive to our client's house, sit with our client, explain the request, discuss our possible response, and drive back to our office to draft one. Once drafted, we would return to our client's house for their final approval, as you would do with any other client. Once approved, the response was sent to Washington. It would now be past midnight for an eight o'clock in the morning deadline for response. We spent many similar sleepless nights because of these government tactics. It was astonishing to me.

As April 2000 came upon us, with Easter right around the corner, we received an incredibly positive legal opinion from the Eleventh Circuit Court of Appeals granting us a temporary injunction prohibiting the federal government from removing Elián from the United States. Injunctions are granted only after a court determines that you are likely to prevail on the merits of your claim. After reading the injunction, we felt cautiously optimistic about the ultimate outcome of our case. One can only assume that when the injunction was read in D.C., they reached a similar conclusion.

The injunction was issued on the Wednesday before Easter Sunday, and it set off the events that would eventually lead to Elián being forcibly removed at gunpoint from his Miami home during a Holy Saturday pre-dawn raid.

Janet Reno was born and raised in Miami and had served as our state attorney. We all knew her and she knew us. On Thursday, Reno sent some mutual friends to meet with us: Aaron Podhurst—a prominent Miami attorney who was close to her; Tad Foote, president of the University of Miami; and two prominent Cuban businessmen, Carlos de la Cruz and Carlos Saladrigas. They expressed to us their profound interest in assisting us to find a solution that took into account the best interests of Elián and of the community. Their mission was to seek a settlement that would resolve this matter in a mutually agreeable way. I explained to them that we had gone down this path before with others. In fact, I had personally spoken to Reno several times about the matter. Every time it appeared that a resolution was possible, something would change. It seemed to us that there was no acceptable settlement for the federal government outside court.

Our offer to settle was very simple. Juan Miguel González was already in the United States. We wanted the family to meet alone at a neutral site, without lawyers or politicians, without interference from the U.S. or Cuban governments. We thought that if the family came together inside a room, yelled at each other a little bit, and made a decision, they could come out and tell the rest of us what they wanted, and we would all honor their wishes. Neither Reno nor Castro would ever agree to this scenario. All we can surmise is that the other side, led by Gregory Craig (the lawyer representing Elián's father), or Fidel Castro— you pick—would object. We had concluded that they didn't want any kind of resolution. The only resolution acceptable to them was for Elián to return to Cuba. Yet, because Podhurst, Foote, Saladrigas, and de la Cruz were friends, and because it was in Elián 's best interests, we agreed to try once more. We expressed our shared concerns and welcomed their help. We embarked on a new round of conversations. This is now, as I mentioned, Thursday of Holy Week.

On the morning of Good Friday, we convened in our law office to work out an agreement. Aaron Podhurst and the group of four presented us with a six-point proposal that had been blessed by countless other community leaders and by the attorney general herself. Aaron was on the phone back and forth with Janet Reno to make sure everything was acceptable. By noon, we had reached an agreement, which had been approved by Reno.

At its core, the agreement included a requirement that the family meet at a neutral site to discuss Elián's future without any outside interference whatsoever. We asked Elián 's family to join us for lunch so we could explain the agreement and they agreed to the terms of the settlement. To satisfy the attorney general that the family was acting in good faith, we were told to initially fax an unsigned copy of the pre-approved proposal to the attorney general by 5:00 P.M., and to obtain the signatures of Lázaro, Marisleysis, and Delfín González subsequently. At 4:52, the attorney general received the fax. Immediately thereafter, we rushed to the González home and obtained the required signatures. We had complied with all her requests.

Now it's 5:00 P.M. on Good Friday. Aaron confirmed that we had a deal. He and President Foote went home, assuming we had a deal. Kendall, Saladrigas and de la Cruz returned with me to the González home to await official confirmation. Presumably, only the agreement of Greg Craig and his client stood in the way of a final resolution.

It started getting late and still no word. I spent most of the night sitting outside the home on Elián 's swing set, enjoying the evening air. Throughout the evening, I was in constant contact with Aaron, the attorney general's close friend. He, in turn, was in constant contact with the attorney general. I would phone Aaron occasionally. What's going on? His response was always the same. Nothing. Just hang in there. Don't go to sleep. You'll be hearing from me soon. Just wait. I would report our conversation each time to all inside the house.

By all indications, our negotiations seemed to be proceeding smoothly. In fact, during one of the calls, Aaron told me, "I can't get into this in great detail with you, but if the other side does not agree to the deal soon, you'll be very pleased with what she [Reno] is going to say." That was the first time I actually felt like my government was on my side, as opposed to seemingly doing Castro's bidding. For the first time ever during the course of the case, I felt a sense of relief. Again, I went inside the house and relayed my recent conversation with Aaron. Believing the end was near, that our deal was still in place, that a resolution now seemed within reach, everyone went to sleep, except me. I kept rocking on the swing outside. We continued to wait.

At approximately 4:00 A.M. disaster struck. I received another call from a dejected Aaron. I was hoping this would be his final call to me, the one that confirmed that all parties were in agreement. Instead, a completely different conversation followed. In a distraught and nervous tone, he explained that the attorney general was no longer in agreement with the pre-approved proposal. In fact, the attorney general was adding new conditions never before discussed. Moreover, after waiting nearly twelve grueling hours for a response, Aaron announced that she wanted an immediate response.

"What's wrong?" I asked.

Aaron didn't know what changed since our last hopeful conversation. All he knew was that there were a set of new conditions that required the immediate approval of the family. We had gone from a signed pre-approved deal to an ultimatum. I asked, "What do you expect me to do now?" He said, "They want an answer, and they want an answer now." I reminded him that he too was a lawyer. There was no possible way we could respond that quickly at this hour of the morning. He knew how intense and emotional this matter had been for all concerned. And I thought we had a deal.

I advised Aaron that after waiting so many hours for a response, Lazaro and Marisleysis, after suffering through yet another day of government threats and ultimatums, had gone to sleep. In fact, everyone had gone to sleep, believing that we had a deal with the government. How in the world can anyone realistically expect me to wake up the family at 4:00 A.M. to advise them that the deal is off and that there was a whole new set of conditions that they must approve within a few minutes. You would never ever treat any other client this way. When was the last time you called a client at four in the morning to tell them a deal you had negotiated had changed?

Aaron replied, "I'm sorry it has changed; I know this is terrible."

"I thought we had a deal, please don't ask me to wake them up now," I said. "If anything, I'm tired myself. I've been up all night; at least allow me to go home, shower, shave and put on a new set of clothes. Let everybody sleep and I'm more than willing to reconvene the group at my office in a few hours, at seven or eight o'clock in the morning. We can then under more reasonable and dignified conditions, including the benefit of a client who had at least a couple of hours of sleep, determine why the government has reneged on their agreement and consider the new conditions."

"Sounds reasonable, I'll get back to you," Aaron said.

Just moments later, Aaron called me back for the last time.

"No, they need an answer in five minutes."

Five minutes! Again I plead with Aaron, this is not right.

But Aaron said no, you have no choice but to wake them up.

I agreed. As their lawyer, I now had no choice but to wake them up and inform them of the new developments. And so I did.

In retrospect, the reality was that the government wanted everybody awake for other reasons. Armed government agents were already on their way. The raid had been set in motion. Breaking into a house where everyone is suddenly awakened from their sleep could no doubt have created a dangerous situation.

Aaron and I kept talking. I turned on the speaker on my cell phone so the entire group could now join in the conversation. After explaining the attorney general's new conditions to this exhausted family, we continued to explore and discuss various options with the family. At the same time, we all continued to plead with Aaron that he secure the agreement of the attorney general not to force a decision now, but that we instead reconvene a little later in the morning. It was very possible that we would agree to some of the new conditions. For example, an agreement to move the neutral site where the families would meet to an out of state location was feasible. However, five in the morning was not a reasonable time to have this discussion and all we asked was to be provided a few hours to rest before we reconvened.

At approximately 5:00 A.M., while still on the phone with Aaron, who was mediating with the attorney general, I suddenly heard loud screaming outside. Because it was Good Friday, most of the people who had kept a constant vigil around the house had left, believing a deal was in place and also thinking that our government would never consider an armed raid on the house, especially not during a religious holiday.

When the media had asked me for a status report earlier that evening, I told them that we had made significant progress and were close to a final deal. People had heard this and went home. Although the hundreds of people who usually stood outside the house had left, one small group remained; a group of very religious Cuban American women who dressed in black and held prayer vigils every night. Two of them were Mrs. de la Cruz and Mrs. Saladrigas. When the Ninja-looking federal security forces arrived, they threw these ladies to the ground.

When I heard the screaming, my worst fears were confirmed. The last words I said to Aaron were, "They're here. The feds are here." Aaron said, "What?" And then we were cut off.

The agents used some sort of ramming device to burst through the front door, pointed machine guns at us and used tear gas. I'm not sure if they gassed the inside the house, or if the tear gas that was stinging our eyes came from outside. In any case the tear gas filled the very small house. The world remembers the picture: the one in which a terrified Elián is held in the arms of Donato Dalrymple (one of the fishermen who had rescued Elián) as a federal agent in goggles and helmet points an automatic weapon at the boy. The armed men then grabbed Elián and rushed him into a waiting van.

We had always allowed an Associated Press photographer to station himself right outside the front door of the house. We never truly wanted to believe that a government raid was ever possible. But if it were to happen, we wanted to make sure it was documented. That is the only reason that famous picture exists. The cameraman was able to work his way into the house as the agents broke through the door. In the confusion, the armed agents had no idea he was going to be there snapping the now famous photo. On the other hand, a television cameraman from the local ABC station was not as fortunate. He too tried to follow the armed agents into the house. However, he was stopped and given a blow to his head that left him bleeding and required stitches.

Janet Reno knew we were in the house; she could have secured a warrant or court order compelling us to hand over custody of Elián, an order we would have no choice but to obey. We had warned the family of this eventuality, and they fully understood. There was no knock. Although we would later learn that they had secured a warrant the night before the raid, no court order or warrant was ever produced for the entry. Instead, we encountered just brute force by armed agents against unarmed civilians, including a child. They surrounded the house, rammed down the door, took Elián at gunpoint, and that was it.

We were in utter shock. We couldn't believe what had happened. We threw water in our faces, trying to relieve the effects of the tear gas. People outside were crying. It was a state of complete confusion and mayhem. After several efforts, I was able to call my family on my cell phone to let them know I was okay. The city was quickly abuzz since the media had some skeleton crews in place that began filming immediately. Those who were up at five in the morning saw the coverage, and started calling their relatives and friends. Soon everyone knew about what had happened.

Kendall and I went to the office and prepared a letter to Janet Reno, expressing our complete and utter disgust at what had just happened. We reminded her that there was an injunction, that the government could not take Elián out of the country, since that would be in direct contravention of a court order. What Reno and the U.S. government could not accomplish in the courts, they accomplished with violent force. It was a case of might makes right.

After we sent the letter, we kept working through Easter Sunday. I was physically and emotionally drained. I couldn't believe that this could take place in my country. It was contrary to everything I had ever learned in a government or civics class or during law school. How do you justify the raid? Those are the kinds of acts you read about in other countries that don't respect the rule of law, but not in ours.

Government officials put Elián on a plane and flew him to his father, who had arrived in the United States on April 6. Soon photos started to emerge showing Elián smiling, laughing and playing with his father. All this was by design, of course. We never gave up, but knew that once these images were widely disseminated, there was, realistically, very little chance we would succeed in the court of public opinion, and even in a court of law. For all practical purposes, at that point, the case was over.

We made our arguments before the Eleventh Circuit Court of Appeals, but apparently the well-reasoned legal analysis that had supported the Court's issuance of the temporary injunction was no longer persuasive. We then appealed to the U.S. Supreme Court. We believed that we had some very compelling legal arguments, relying on a long line of abolitionist cases serving as precedent. We also pointed to conflicts between appellate districts; another basis for the Supreme Court to have agreed to hear our case (in our case, it was conflict between the Ninth and Eleventh Circuit Courts). The Supreme Court, however, refused to hear our case.

Very soon, in June 2000, Elián was flown back to Cuba. Despite our repeated requests, the family that had cared for and nurtured Elián during these very difficult months was never allowed to visit him before the return to Cuba. They have not been able to visit him since.

We never received an official reason from Janet Reno or the U.S. government as to why they seized Elián. It was clear no one cared. I had spent most of my life defending the rights of others, always believing that in the greatest country in the world fairness, justice, and the rule of law are greater than any one person or institution. At 5:00 A.M., on April 22, 2000, Janet Reno and the U.S. Department of Justice circumvented the rule of law, put our lives in danger, and trampled on the rights of a group of Americans. This was not the America I grew up in, the America I love.

Chapter 5 The Choice for Change

IN FALL 2000, I formally decided to run for mayor of Miami. It wasn't a spur-of-the-moment decision.

After the raid on Elián's home, I witnessed the expression of many of the same feelings in our community so prevalent in the aftermath of the Mariel boatlift. News reports showed African Americans standing next to white Americans holding a Confederate flag yelling "Cubans go home." This was a stark reminder of a time and place I had fought so hard to move us beyond. Much in the same way that in 1980 I went back on my personal promise not to become involved in political and community issues at the expense of my professional career, in 2000 I decided that I again had to act. I had to do something. I chose to run for mayor of Miami, but not as a first step in a long political career—rather, because Miami is our brand and the mayor has the bully pulpit, I believed that this was the best place to effect change, to bring people back together.

In Miami, mayoral elections are nonpartisan. I ran as an independent. A lifelong registered Democrat, I had switched to independent as my own personal protest of the illegal raid that snatched Elián and of a party that no longer seemed to represent the ideals that had long inspired me. My decision to switch parties, to run as an Independent, was totally unrelated to my decision to campaign for office.

I first sought my family's blessing. They were all very supportive. I spoke to some friends, both old childhood friends and many others whose opinions I valued and whose support I wanted and needed. The reactions ranged from "you're crazy" to "yes, we will support you," even though it might be a real uphill battle. But it didn't matter, we were friends.

I began to assemble a campaign team and called Al Lorenzo, an old high school friend I had played baseball with when we were kids. I asked him to be my campaign manager. I also called one of the lawyers in our office who is now my law partner, Richard Lydecker, and he became my finance director. We started working on a targeted fundraising list and I opened a campaign bank account. I established the account in mid-December and set a goal of raising $200,000 by December 31, the end of the first financial reporting period. This was a very difficult time to raise money. Not only were we in the middle of the holidays, but we had just completed a very expensive presidential election.

We wanted to get out of the box in January with a very strong showing and we did, raising just over $200,000 in three weeks. Running as an independent was not a negative in terms of fundraising. One of the benefits of most mayoral elections is that people don't ask your party affiliation. They generally don't care, contributing instead on the basis of whether you will be a good mayor. Raising such a large amount of money so quickly received a lot of attention in the media. We sent a message and people took note of the fact that this would be a serious campaign, albeit from an untested candidate.

My early fund-raising success can be largely attributed to some dear old friends and to the statewide contacts developed through years of raising money for Democratic candidates. Absent from my list were the typical donors, people I knew from the business community of Miami, and who had already made commitments to either the incumbent or one of the prior incumbents in the race. The first group I drew on—my old friends from Belen, my doctor and lawyer friends going back to when we were kids—never realized they could be prolific fundraisers. Most had never written a single political campaign check. Our local newspaper, the *Miami Herald*, found it difficult to determine my source of contributions. The reporters couldn't do a cross-check with previous fundraising records because this group had not donated before (normally this kind of cross-checking turns up the usual suspects who donate). I remember the *Herald* initial reports suggesting that I was receiving considerable money from the "health industry"—which, in reality, consisted of my Belen doctor friends.

My other fundraising source included friends and fellow fundraisers from around the State of Florida. Friends such as insurance executives Charley Lydecker (Richard's brother) from Ormond Beach (a Democrat) and Tony Grippa, then a Republican county commissioner from Leon County (Tallahassee), proved invaluable in raising funds from Tallahassee, the Tampa Bay area, Orlando, Daytona Beach, and Broward County. This is why I was able to raise the early money, and how I kept pace with the other candidates as the campaign progressed. In fact, it turned out to be an expensive race, setting a fundraising record for that time.

During this period, we also started defining our campaign message. The city had experienced a decade of constant financial and political turmoil. My message was simple: I was the choice for change. I grew up in Miami, went to school in Miami, worked in Miami. I was a successful businessman, not a career politician. I could bring people together. I could create political stability. I also spoke about specific issues such as education and infrastructure—issues that the city had done absolutely nothing about. I focused on the need to create jobs, build our economy, and create a great urban core. These were the concerns I talked about. That was the message.

Our focus was entirely positive. I never attacked Joe Carollo, the incumbent mayor, who was running for reelection. The field I ran against consisted of nine candidates, including all the mayors from 1973 through 2001—Ferre, Xavier Suarez, and Carollo—with the exception of Steve Clark, who was elected in November 1995 and passed away the following year. The field also included an incumbent City of Miami commissioner and a former city manager.

Many in Miami were critical of Carollo. Frankly, I thought he had done some good things as mayor. I would constantly remind people that I was not interested in running against him. I thought he had done the best he could, but now the city needed to move forward, move to the next level. And I could take it there. None of the candidates really attacked me. They didn't consider me a threat.

After my strong financial showing, one of my opponents, Maurice Ferre, whom I would ultimately face in a runoff, released a poll that showed me at 3 percentage points. When you factor in the margin of error, I could have been at minus 1 percent! In fact, my own polling confirmed that I was about 3 percent, but obviously I was not sharing my results with anyone, or so I thought. The release of that poll result was a strategic effort by Maurice to take a huge shot across the bow of my campaign. The ability to raise money gives an air of credibility to any campaign. But the ability to continue to raise money is dealt a severe blow when a poll shows you can't win. Sure, your immediate group of friends will continue to give you money simply because you are a friend. Others have a different view: Why give money to a candidate with no chance? You're so far behind you'll never catch up.

In a way, however, the poll was also a blessing in disguise. My opponents wrote me off, thinking I would never break the 3 percent mark. They didn't track my progress, they didn't see that I was walking door-to-door, visiting up to 700 houses in a week. They didn't realize that I was building up this support at the grassroots level, little by little, day by day, hour by hour, until the very end. Toward the end of the race, the *Miami Herald* and other media sources released their own polls. By that point, I was among the front runners, still in the middle rear of the pack, but in the pack. Suddenly, I became a real candidate again, one to be reckoned with. And this is exactly the optimal time to peak. It is really only near the end of a race that the general public starts to pay close attention to the election and the candidates. In March, April, and May, who is thinking about the election? In September they certainly are, and in October people really start to focus. And this is when you want to hit your stride.

With such a large field of candidates, a runoff was inevitable. There simply was no way that any one candidate would receive 50 percent +1 of the vote and win without a runoff. Thus, our strategy focused on making the runoff: being one of the two top vote-getters. This was no easy task. My opponents had almost all either held office or been involved in city government. They all had name recognition and built in constituencies. They each had a base of support. When you combine their starting base, their support could be greater than 60 to 70 percent. This left little room for a new guy. Our goal was to chip away at everybody's base, little by little, at the same time that we also tried to capture the vote of those who were not committed to any candidate.

During my "stealth" campaign door to door, people would often tell me that "I've got to vote for Carollo," the incumbent, or "We're voting for Maurice Ferre," one of the prior mayors, because they or their families knew each other or had some connection to the candidate from their years in office. In those cases I would ask, "If they don't make the runoff, can I have your support?" I wanted to become their second choice. Through my campaign database, I was able to identify for both the general and runoff elections those who had indicated their willingness to vote for me and those who would support me if their first choice did not make the runoff.

As I visited more and more homes, our message kept getting better and better, since it reflected more of what I learned from the people I was meeting. Walking door to door is an important tool for winning an election. But just as important, if not more so, it makes you a better candidate. You are actually talking to people, day in, day out, six to ten hours a day—which is the only way you can walk to as many homes as I did—10,000. I would start walking on a weekday afternoon until dark, about eight in the evening, if not later at times. On weekends, both Saturday and Sunday, I would start around ten in the morning and continue until eight at night. I would break off when it looked like it was just too late to knock on someone's door. I visited all Miami's neighborhoods. I learned the issues, learned what was on people's minds, what they cared about, and what they wanted to see in a mayor. I learned about their fears, their hopes. The other candidates were not talking with the people I had spoken to in my stealth campaign—people whose houses were flooding because of infrastructure problems in the city, whose kids were attending bad schools because education was not a focus for city government. People wanted to hear how I was going improve their schools, fix their streets, make their neighborhoods safer, help improve police-community relations.

Ours was an unconventional campaign. My political flyers were also unconventional. The first piece of mail we sent was, in essence, a photo album meant to introduce me to the voters. There was a picture of me as a baby in a little bathtub and as a young boy dressed in a cowboy outfit. You can walk into any Cuban household and find similar pictures. It also included a photo of a Pan Am airplane, a symbol of the Cuban freedom flights to the United States. There was also a picture of me wearing my graduation cap and gown with my family, a symbol of the American Dream.

These were my personal pictures. They represented my life. No issues, yet. Framing who you are, before opponents do so, is essential to any campaign—and a key to winning. Voters want to be able to relate to you personally before they focus on what you stand for. This helps you gain credibility, making it easier to get the message across.

I prepared a postcard I would mail to voters immediately after I visited their homes. The postcard had some preprinted text and a picture of me on the front and perhaps one of my family members as well. On the back, the card was divided in half. On the right side was the address, and on the left a preprinted message depending on whether the person I had met was voting for me or for an opponent or was undecided. Whatever the reaction, I had a card to match it. I supplemented that text with a handwritten note that captured some element of our visit, something the voter told me, or what I had seen in the neighborhood or in their home. This was an important way of personalizing my visit. I would write a personal note at the bottom of the card such as "I am sorry about your flooding problems and I promise you I am going to do everything I can to fix it." If it was a casual conversation and someone mentioned a personal matter—for instance, that their grandson was in the finals for the spelling bee—I would add a little note saying "I wish your grandson luck. I'm sure he'll win." The point was to always personalize the visit, to let the voter know that I remembered something unique about them and listened.

This is much more than the typical, "I was at your house" impersonal postcard that many politicians who walk door-to-door would often leave behind. On my return visits to many of these same homes, I was humbled to find that people were keeping my postcards, attached with a magnet to the refrigerator, and in some cases, framed. In many of these homes, I was fed. I ate black beans, red beans, croquettes, and other delicacies that to this day remain a delicious mystery. I was making a special connection with the voters.

▢ ▢ ▢

THE NIGHT OF the general election was tense. We knew Maurice Ferre would be in the runoff. The remaining question was who would be his opponent. As predicted, Ferre led with 31.4 percent of the vote, I took second with 23.7, and Joe Carollo, incumbent mayor, had 23.2 percent. Only 236 votes separated Carollo and me. It appeared our strategy had worked. What was once a contest of nine people was now down to two. The runoff election was scheduled for seven days later.

Because of the slim margin, Carollo had a right to a recount. Based on the political history of Miami, we all assumed he would ask for a recount. Had he challenged the results, it would have changed the dynamics of the race dramatically. Essentially, it would have prevented both of us from campaigning or raising money, while Ferre could continue to do both. Instead, Carollo ultimately endorsed me in the runoff. Another helpful endorsement came from the *Miami Herald*. In my effort to build credibility, the *Herald* endorsement was especially important for the white non-Hispanic community, the largest demographic of the paper's circulation.

The week between the general election and the runoff was a blur of debates and intensive efforts to fundraise. You can't raise money on Tuesday, because that's election day. That meant we only had Wednesday and Thursday to fundraise since the cut-off was Thursday night. In those intense two days, we managed to raise $400,000. There was no time for formal fundraising events, so people were asked to show up and drop off their contributions at the banquet hall of a local restaurant where we had set up shop. Meanwhile, I was out debating my opponent, starting at 8:00 A.M., the day after the election. We engaged in at least a dozen major debates during the runoff. Toward the end of the week, I constantly had a bottle of water and honey at my side because I had literally lost my voice. It was a whirlwind.

Maurice had been mayor for twelve years, had a generally good reputation with the voters and was also well financed. He was running on his past record, on his past experience. During the debates, Maurice would mock me, especially on the issue of education. Traditionally, mayors in Miami had nothing to do with education. The Miami-Dade County School Board is a separate body, with its own governance and administration. Mayors did not have authority or a connection to it. But education was one of the central concerns I would hear from voters whose homes I visited. Parents with young children would ask me: "Do we move out because the school here in our neighborhood is terrible?" I knew that education was on the minds of the parents I met. And for me education is something I am personally invested in. It was my key out of poverty. Instinctively I knew it, personally I had gone through it, and, as I walked door to door, I was seeing and hearing more and more about it. I knew it was important.

Maurice, however, would attack me. "Manny is being a demagogue. He knows mayors have nothing to do with education." But Maurice was out of touch. That was an entirely wrong thing to say in front of a group of people, especially parents, who were no doubt thinking, "Well, maybe the mayor should do something about education! Maybe Manny is on to something here." I don't think any mayoral candidate in Miami ever ran on a platform with education as one of its planks, until I did it.

Other issues drew a clear distinction between Maurice and me. One of them was infrastructure. I remember walking neighborhoods where residents told me it had been thirty to forty years since their streets had been fixed. In some cases I saw a City of Miami Public Works truck arrive to fill a pothole with eight guys in the truck. They would get out, throw some gravel into the hole, pack it, and leave. I would stand there and think, "I'm no engineer, but something tells me that hole's not fixed." As soon as a few cars drove over the patchwork, the hole reappeared. One neighbor called her street Dalmatian Street since it had so many black holes. If you walk through this neighborhood today, you will see that all the streets have been repaired.

Sidewalks torn up, swales nonexistent or muddy or flooding: that's what I saw firsthand as I walked Miami's many neighborhoods. The city had started in the east, along the Miami River, and as it moved west it had not built the infrastructure necessary to accommodate this growth. No parks: most of the city's parks are in the east. No attempts to control flooding: again, most of the city's pump stations were located in the eastern part of the city.

After I was elected, I received a call from people in one particular neighborhood. They wanted me to visit their street, so I could personally experience their difficulties with flooding. I drove over right away. It was so bad I had to borrow rubber boots from the fire department to walk with the district commissioner, Angel Gonzalez, down that street. Today, that same street no longer floods. Working in partnership with Commissioner Gonzalez, we invested significant time, effort, and resources to mitigate flooding problems in many of these neighborhoods, so much so that by the time we both left office, few, if any, flooding complaints would be received in our respective offices.

Residents in another neighborhood told me during the campaign that they would not put furniture on their front porch or in their foyer because that part of the house would flood whenever it rained. It was a way of life. They had put up with this forever. No one was ever going to do anything about this, so why complain, they said. Their solution was not to put any furniture in the entire front part their house. Imagine that! Today, that street no longer floods. So, when I raised the issue of infrastructure during the debates, talked about the need to invest in flood mitigation, fix our streets, and fix our parks, it came from firsthand knowledge, from hearing what people had to say.

I also understood the importance of parks in keeping kids out of trouble. With my parents working two jobs, I am sure they felt comfort knowing I was at a city park with an adult supervisor who took care of me while they were at work. Sadly, by the time I ran for office, the parks I grew up in were now home to drug deals and other criminal activity. Needles littered the ground. You couldn't go into a park—you didn't want to. In one instance, I discovered a park where the city itself was dumping construction debris and oil. When I became mayor, we cleaned this area and built a beautiful new park.

There were signs everywhere of a city that no longer cared. Voters were the ones who told me to look at their parks, look at their streets, and look at how filthy their neighborhoods had become. They kept their homes orderly. You didn't walk in and see a pile of trash in their living room. Why didn't the city do the same? The city should look like their home: orderly and clean. Instead, people believed no one cared. They had lost hope. They got used to water flooding their homes because they felt no one cared. Why get upset about it? Nobody cares, no one is ever going to do anything about it. That had become the prevailing attitude.

Crime was another issue people talked about, but it wasn't a dominant issue. What people did talk about was about their complete distrust for the police department. The city had experienced a number of police shootings involving African Americans as well other cases involving police abuse. I knew instinctively and from past experience that I would get some pushback with regard to the police department in the black community. I did not think I would hear the same concerns in the Cuban community or the Latino community, which had traditionally been very supportive of law enforcement. Yet that was not the case. Much of the mistrust had to do with the police reaction post-Elián. Many people were unjustly mistreated by the police department during the morning after the raid on Elián's home. People standing on street corners would be pushed, hit, and arrested without justification. Poor police-community relations had become a significant issue to be dealt with by the next mayor of Miami.

These were the issues I was talking about—those that mattered most to people, all the while drawing a very clear distinction with Maurice. He was part of the problem. I was bringing the solutions. Ferre also made a huge tactical error. He was accustomed to winning by building coalitions of voting blocs of ethnic and racial groups, very often at the expense of dividing and pitting one group against another.

I started with 3 percent and now I was in the runoff. How should Ferre counter me? He decided to raise Elián. I never spoke about Elián during the general campaign. When the media asked, I would refuse to answer. I never wanted to connect running for office with work on behalf of Elián.

Ferre always held his own with the Hispanic vote and was very strong with the black vote. However, he was no doubt surprised by how well I had done with the white non-Hispanic vote. He surmised that if he could keep his Hispanic base and get overwhelming majorities of blacks and Anglos, he could win. Using Elián was a way to remind blacks and Anglos that I had played a significant role in this issue that had divided our community. He was using a polarizing issue to suit his political goal: winning. As a result, my share of the black and non-Hispanic white vote in the runoff was lowered somewhat. What he didn't count on was the massive adverse negative reaction he received from Miami's Hispanic community, the largest voting bloc in the city. By attacking me, he attacked Elián, a major political mistake in a community still very much hurting from the experience.

Election day, November 13. Exit polls showed me winning by 10 percentage points. When the polls closed, the first precincts to report were largely Ferre strongholds. He appeared to be winning and, as a result, those around me became very nervous. I kept reassuring them, "We're going to win. Remember, in 1984, I was the first guy to do exit polling in Miami, so I know exit polling and I trust exit polling." No one believed me. Not much later, the race was called in my favor. The final numbers: 55.3 percent for me, 44.7 percent for Ferre.

Maurice never called me to concede.

I was sworn in as mayor of Miami on November 18, five days after the election. That also set a new precedent. Joe Carollo called me after I won and asked, "Do you mind if I have a few days to pack up?" This may seem an odd question to many, but in prior Miami elections, the winning candidate and his supporters would drive to City Hall at midnight with a moving truck that same evening. The next day, in the Commission Chambers, he would be sworn in as mayor. I asked Carollo how many days he needed and he said five. I agreed and this became the norm.

I was sworn in on a Saturday. We held the ceremony outdoors, with tents and bleachers, rather than inside City Hall. I wanted it to take place on the weekend to give people who work during the week a chance to participate. My campaign was unique in its grassroots focus. This is something we have lost in America. Campaigns have become very expensive, very media intensive, and people no longer have a chance to shake the hand of the candidates. They can no longer look a candidate in the eye. Now, it's all about sound bites and the 30-second spots. I love personal campaigns. I love to go out and talk with people, losing twenty pounds in the process. Walking helps you learn so much, and helps crystallize your message as the campaign develops. It helped me get to City Hall, and once I got there, I never forgot what I learned from those walks.

When the campaign starts, you know what you want. When the campaign ends, your success may very well depend on your ability to have listened to and understood what the voters want.

Chapter 6 **Now What?**

I DID NOT RUN for mayor as part of a pre-programmed political career path. I did not run as a stepping stone for future political office. I ran to make a difference because I loved Miami and saw its potential. Miami is the city I grew up in. It is the city that my parents, in their own humble way, helped to build. It is also city made up predominantly of Hispanics, primarily Cuban Americans. If Miami was considered a laughingstock, then by extension, Cuban Americans would be viewed in a similar vein. This could not be the legacy of my parents' generation. Their legacy was becoming one where their children were leaving the city because they saw no future in Miami. I ran to change that.

What was our reputation? What did people know about Miami? Aside from the beautiful weather, great beaches and palm trees, and being a great place to vacation? Miami was the drug capital, the homicide capital, number one in poverty, and home to significant ethnic and racial tensions that had resulted in four major riots during a single decade: a city economically at a standstill, with no new projects under way or planned. Nothing of substance had been built in Miami in years. It was not a place that provided opportunity. It was not a place where people chose to settle and create a life for their families.

Who lived in Miami? People who could not afford to move to the suburbs, a large immigrant population that continued to grow and fight to achieve the American Dream, and an older generation that was settled in and not going anywhere. Some pockets of good neighborhoods could still be found, and there was the urban core, where everyone got to work at nine in the morning and left at five in the evening.

Adding to the list of negatives was a state-appointed financial oversight board and a tremendous amount of political instability at City Hall, which many had renamed "Silly Hall." The media loved publishing stories about the exploits of my predecessors. One former mayor, wearing a bathrobe and PJs, decided to visit a constituent in the middle of the night to confront her for writing a letter to the editor criticizing him. She greeted him at the door with a gun. Another former mayor was involved in a high profile domestic dispute and was accused of throwing a teapot at his wife. There was absentee ballot fraud and dead voters, and a state court had to take the unusual step of removing a newly elected mayor and replacing him with the person he ran against and beat. This was "political leadership" in Miami.

At the same time, I was watching the rebirth of other American cities. Many cities that had declined in the 1960s and 1970s were experiencing a renewal in the 1990s. People were moving back into cities to be part of the urban life. Entrepreneurial mayors in cities like New York, Chicago, Boston, and others ushered in a new era of urban renaissance. Due to a lack of leadership in Miami, this renewal had passed us by. I wanted Miami to join this list of great American cities believing that our potential was equal to or greater than many of these other cities. The Mayor's Office is where everything happens: it is the face of the city.

Obviously, when you take office within five days of an election, there is no transition period. You go right to work. Unfortunately, much of that work in the first few weeks is not especially newsworthy as you begin to build your staff and meet with department directors. The Spanish language *Miami Herald* published a story reviewing my first hundred days in office. The reporter gave me a nickname that stuck with me for a while: "The Invisible Mayor." They said I wasn't doing anything, that I was invisible. I was not invisible. I was busy working.

For most major public offices, there is a period between November and formally taking office in January during which you can be invisible to the larger public and the media as you build your team and establish your priorities. Then, on inauguration day, you start with your agenda. I did not have this luxury.

☐ ☐ ☐

ALL ASPIRING POLITICIANS should be careful what they wish for. I had never seen government from the inside. Although I had been involved in many political campaigns, and obviously knew a lot of people in government, I couldn't prepare myself for what I was about to find.

I had never experienced a culture quite like that of government, where the favorite answer is, "No, it can't be done." No matter what you ask for, the answer is always "no." Then, if you ask why, the answer is, "because that's the way we've always done it," or, better still, "somebody told me to do it this way." I never found this "somebody" in the city's organizational chart, yet clearly this "somebody" had a lot of power.

All this is tied into something called institutional knowledge. As mayor, you are told that you can't make changes in city government because institutional knowledge will suffer. I quickly realized that I didn't want to keep the institutional knowledge that had created the kinds of problems we had in the City of Miami. Nonetheless, the reality is that many bureaucrats would remain in place long after I had moved on. Everyone knows that a mayor is in office for four years, eight with term limits, but bureaucrats may very well be there twenty or thirty years.

This reality can easily co-opt the agenda of an ambitious mayor. When I walked into a meeting and announced, "I've got this cleanup initiative that I really want implemented," everybody around the table would nod their heads and say, "Absolutely Mr. Mayor. Great idea, you know we're on it." You leave the room, move on to a hundred other projects, all the while assuming that your directive would be followed. Six months later you ask, "What happened to my cleanup initiative?" You call everybody back into the room and listen to a whole series of rather creative excuses as to why nothing has been done. I am confident that somebody (there he is again) has written a book entitled something like *101 Excuses to Give the Mayor When Inquiring About His Projects*. After politely (at least at the beginning of your term) listening to an assortment of excuses, you again emphasize the importance of your initiative. You wonder if perhaps they thought you were kidding. The process repeats itself: they once again nod their heads and go through the same routine, often very sincerely. The tactic of city bureaucrats is to beat you down by virtue of sincere non-action in the hope that you'll eventually just give up or forget your agenda. This is why as mayor, if you want to be successful, you just have to outwork everyone. You can't forget or give up.

I also realized that the biggest department in the City of Miami was the "fire department." Why? Every employee in the city was trained to put out fires. Presumably, these were the expectations that had been previously communicated to the employees, perhaps by "somebody." When a constituent calls with a problem, you put out that fire. You don't ever fix any real underlying problems, you manage them day-to-day. This culture permeated not just the rank-and-file city personnel, but also the management level. Keep in mind that many had arrived at management positions not by merit, but simply because they outlasted everybody else in the system. Management would come to me and say, "You know, Mr. Mayor, we picked up the garbage, we handled all citizen complaints, and when you walked into your office this morning and turned on the lights, they worked": putting forth just enough effort. This was supposed to make me happy. This is the reason I sacrificed my private practice and my family life? Ouch!

When you first face this culture, you realize that you are at a serious personal crossroad. There is no going back now. On the one hand, change is difficult. You could decide to coast in office for four years, do a lot of photo ops, and do a couple of good things here and there where there is little resistance. If you do that, there is a good chance that you'll get reelected. It is amazing how many politicians use this very formula to hold on to power for decades. Yet, if you want to make a difference and create meaningful change, you need to fight and overcome the natural resistance of the bureaucracy. You do this by showing them you are sincere about your intent; you incorporate them into your team and then have them buy into your vision.

That is the approach I took. I set a simple goal: to make my city livable, improving the quality of life to bring back the middle-class residents who had moved out and stimulating new private investments to help those citizens who were left behind. Once I made that decision, I started to change the government culture. To do this, I had to change the team. Miami traditionally had a reputation for being very political. Every time a new mayor was elected, everyone was fired. That's not very conducive to a stable, functioning government. So I had to negotiate a delicate balance between trying to find the right way to change the culture and not appearing motivated by purely political considerations. My solution to this problem was to reach out to the private sector. I prioritized an area that government typically overlooks: human resources. I needed a professional who understood the city's needs, the sensitivities of government, and who would still be able to change the culture among some very entrenched employees. We were fortunate to recruit Rosalie Mark, a human resources expert with several decades of private sector experience. She helped build a team of people from outside and within the city who shared a can-do culture, the belief that anything is possible if you just work hard enough.

We also changed the structure of government. We reengineered a number of departments by eliminating some and consolidating others. We created a vertical structure with a chief executive officer, chief financial officer, chief operations officer, chief information officer, and a budget director who was also given the responsibility for strategic fiscal planning.

In most governments, the left hand never knows what the right hand is doing. City departments rarely interface. They would not talk to one another. With this new structure, we changed that considerably. We took the position that there were no sacred cows in city government, including the most basic job descriptions. Everything was open to change. We began to change the bureaucracy. I also had to change the relations between the mayor and the City Commission, the city's legislative body.

Miami has an executive mayor system, a hybrid between a strong and a weak mayor, and I was the first mayor elected under this new structure. One of the powers of the mayor is to run council meetings, or appoint a chair. I chose the latter, rotating the chairmanship annually among the commissioners. In the eight years I served as mayor, I never joined in Commission deliberations. That should be their province. Instead, if I had something to say, I would appear before the commissioners, just like any other member of the public. This included everything from delivering my annual budget address to advocating for a particular issue on their agenda.

I also had the power to veto Commission actions. Not once during my eight years in office did I issue a veto. I met with the commissioners at least every other week, quite often weekly. During our meetings, we discussed the Commission agenda, shared our positions on individual items, and always tried to find consensus. As a result, our Commission meetings were never very contentious, and this also helps to explain why I never had to use my veto power.

It was a two-way street. Ironically, people accused me of manipulating the commissioners, calling them puppets who only did my bidding. This couldn't be farther from the truth. We spent hours vetting all issues, discussing ideas back and forth. Individual commissioners and I very often disagreed. But when we disagreed, we looked for better ways to achieve our goals, behaving instead as true partners always looking for new ways to do what was best for the City of Miami and its residents. It was never a case of me imposing anything on them, never a "vote for this or else."

One of the real benefits of our hybrid form of government is that I could meet with the commissioners one-on-one and discuss agenda matters in private. Florida's Sunshine Law forbids commissioners (and in many cases Florida mayors who are part of the legislative body) to meet among themselves and discuss issues that are, or could appear, before them. Because I was an executive mayor and not a voting member of the Commission, however, I was not subject to these same restrictions. This allowed me to carry out informal discussions with individual commissioners and was hugely important for the effectiveness of city government. By the way, the Florida Legislature, creators of the Sunshine Law, did not impose a similar restriction on themselves. Congress also does not have such a restriction, although in that case it does not seem to matter much anyway.

Think about it this way. People always want government to act more like a business. Business decisions are not shared publicly. If you and your business partners are considering buying a company, do you tell your competition what you are willing to pay for it? This would force you to pay a higher price than you perhaps intended. Do you tell your competition what you're going to do before you do it? Of course not. We saddle government with these restrictions on communications that make it difficult to negotiate in the best interest of the taxpayers.

I understand the reasons behind the Sunshine Law, why people are suspicious and distrustful of government, wanting government actions to be carried out in public. In fact, they are. While all decisions must and should always be made in public, the discussions leading up to those decisions are sometimes best done in private, and should not be prohibited by the Sunshine Law. Under Miami's system of government, the most important position is that of city manager. This was the only employee I had some control over. Still, even if the city manager could count on the support of a majority of the commissioners, he could very well circumvent the mayor's authority. The city manager runs the city, including the hiring and firing of all city employees.

I was not allowed to give directions to any city employees. For example, I could not ask the parks director to start a new parks program. If I saw trash on our streets, I could not call the director of solid waste and threaten his job. That would be a violation of the city charter. I could only speak to the city manager and tell him about the problem. The solution was under his control and discretion.

On taking office, I decided to retain the incumbent city manager, Carlos Giménez, who remained in that position until early 2003. I thought it was important during the transition that I have some stability. That was a very tricky thing for me. On the one hand, I wanted change. And I knew change had to come. Yet, I did not want to appear to be the typical Miami politician who came in and removed a lot of people and replaced them with his friends.

Although hiring decisions were exclusively vested with the city manager, it was important for me to meet with all who wanted to be part of our new team. I wanted to make sure they understood my vision. Miami had to change, and I wanted to build a team that could help me change the city—in every respect. We ended up putting together a great team. I also had to make sure I hired my own staff for the mayor's office. I named François Illas as my chief of staff. François started to put together his team. They were mostly young, in their twenties and thirties. The local newspaper wrote a story about how my staff was too young and inexperienced to get anything done. But I wanted people who were not about to embed themselves in City Hall for twenty or thirty years. I wanted people full of energy and passion for change, committed to public service, who would be with me for as long as I could hold them, before they moved on.

Two positions were essential hires for my vision. But when I reviewed my office budget, adopted prior to my arrival, the funds did not match my priorities. In fact, these positions were not part of any of my predecessors' budgets. First, I needed my own finance person. Right after I was elected, I asked the city manager to arrange a meeting with the budget director, Linda Haskins. She gave me a presentation on the city's finances. It was very clear that the budget would be a huge issue, because understanding the city's finances, even for someone who had dealt with financial issues before, would be a real challenge. You could spend the entire four years of your term trying to figure out government accounting and the city's finances. Shortly after our meeting, Linda quit. I strongly suspected, having just met her for a few hours, that she was quitting out of frustration. She was quitting because she hit a wall every time she tried to tell someone in the city about something that she thought was important. I called Linda at home and explained that I knew why she had quit. I wanted her to come back, this time to work in the mayor's office. She agreed.

Next, I needed my own economic development person. I hired Otto Boudet-Murias. During his tenure, he would become largely responsible for building the new Miami. Because I came from the business community, I knew I needed someone who spoke the language of business. I needed someone in my administration from the business world. I know there are exceptions, but as a general rule, in government those charged with promoting and overseeing economic development generally lack the requisite training and skills to succeed. They are also missing two very fundamental private sector qualities: incentive and the courage to take risks.

Businesspeople understand this. They understand the profit motive; they understand how far you can push in terms of demands and still make a deal attractive enough so that one party doesn't walk away and invest elsewhere. Those who have never been in that world don't understand it. Economic development is not something learned in a class. It takes people with real life experience. I needed someone from that world, and that was Otto.

Because I had no funding for Linda's or Otto's positions, I had to ask the City Commission for a midyear increase to my office budget. They granted my request and this remains one of the best decisions I made during my term. Linda would later become the city's chief financial officer as well as city commissioner. Otto would become the chief economic development officer and later return to the private sector.

□ □ □

WITH A NEW team in place, we set out to further refine ourselves internally. Before we could execute a vision, we needed to get our own house in order. So, we looked top to bottom, and nothing was sacred. We started turning our vision into reality and developed the city's first-ever strategic plan, setting three main goals:

1. Operate as a service-focused organization.
2. Invest in neighborhood and environmental quality.
3. Improve the health and economic development of the city.

I was astonished that the city had never adopted such a plan. This was yet another of the many distinguishing factors I found between my previous private sector experience and government. With a plan, you can communicate expectations to employees, monitor their performance, and hold them accountable through a balanced scorecard methodology—a report card that grades every employee according to what is expected of them. This aligns every employee with one consolidated purpose. Everyone is now pulling in the same direction and knows where they fit into the vision—from the city manager and other supervisors down to the employees pruning trees in our parks.

Before this strategic plan was adopted, city workers did not necessarily understand their role in the greater vision. For example, a parks employee directed to prune three trees would go home at the end of the day not appreciating the significance and importance of the job. With the plan in place, a parks employee prunes three trees as part of a greater goal: we want great parks because great parks make a better city that attracts new people. The employee now understands his role in getting to this goal. Our parks improved so dramatically, they became nationally recognized, and more important, vibrant centers of community and family life.

Next, we combined our goals and expectations with multiyear financial planning to align resources with vision. City budgets were no longer prepared by taking last year's numbers plus or minus 5 percent, as is the practice of most governments. Instead, we began to align our fiscal resources to our needs. The budget reflected our priorities. Resources had to be provided that gave employees the tools needed to achieve the vision we had for the city. With great expectations, we needed to give them the chance and the tools to succeed.

We then engaged in a top-to-bottom rewrite of our business processes, prioritized and created new training programs, and commissioned for the first time ever an information technology strategic plan that replaced an obsolete mainframe system. If we were to compete as a service focused organization, we needed to invest in the latest tools and technology. After becoming a service-focused organization where employees knew what was expected, had the tools, and had resources aligned with our goals, we could now begin our ambitious investment in our neighborhoods.

Chapter 7 **Grand Ideas**

PEOPLE IN GOVERNMENT no longer have grand ideas. When I was a young boy and President John F. Kennedy said we would go to the moon, many people thought he was crazy. Less than ten years later, I sat with my parents and watched on TV as Neil Armstrong landed the Apollo 11 spacecraft on the moon, taking those first historic steps. This image has always stayed with me. Dream big; then lead others to your idea.

When, as mayor, I closed my eyes and imagined the Miami of twenty or thirty years in the future, I knew exactly what I wanted it to look like. Now, it was a matter of getting there.

There were detractors everywhere. The media accused me of being too much of a visionary, too ambitious. They were used to cruise control mayors. So-called "activists" emerged from all over, claiming I was too "big picture," that I didn't care about the little guy. They missed the point that the "big picture" is made up of the smallest details. It most definitely includes fixing a pothole and planting a tree: small details are a part of a larger picture that creates a beautiful and livable city. The bureaucracy also tested me; they tried to wear me down.

I remember giving my first annual state of the city address a few months after taking office. We would take on the challenges that faced Miami, challenges that might not be solved in four or eight years, or even during my lifetime, but we had to start. Here came a grand idea: I wanted Miami to become a city where poverty is not a lifelong condition. That was the key challenge.

When I explained this approach at the Harvard John F. Kennedy School of Government—where I was lecturing as a visiting fellow after my term in office—I remember a student telling me that ours was the most comprehensive approach to government he had ever heard—especially when condensed to forty-five minutes! Students at the school were taught to pick three issues, be known for them, and move on. I cannot be a three-issue person. The notion that I would give up the comfortable life of a big city lawyer to tackle just three issues makes no sense to me; it is a waste of time. My sense of public service is to help people, give them better lives: Men for Others. Public service and government is not about acquiring power, finding the next office to hold, perpetuating your existence. Yet, this is how many politicians and people in government see service. This is governing for the next election, not for the next generation.

To borrow a popular metaphor, government misses the forest for the trees. Government operates in silos, in isolation. It does not communicate and often pulls in different directions. I could very well adopt "flood mitigation" as a priority and construct a pump station near the homes of the people I visited during my campaign that would fix their flooding problems. I could have shown up, taken a picture, cut a ribbon, and kept my promise to prevent water from entering their homes. By most measures, this is a success. The media would announce, "Diaz fixes neighborhood flooding." But how would this contribute to the greater vision? What good is this one "achievement" if the people who live in those homes continue to lack economic opportunity? What if their neighborhood is not as safe and clean as it can be? One thing in isolation is not enough. And I did not want to wait until "my next term" to take on these challenges.

TO GET MIAMI to the place I wanted it to be, we needed to focus and invest in five areas: expanding economic opportunity; making neighborhoods safe; investing in our future; designing a sustainable city; and fostering arts and culture. Taken together, these areas would help create the Miami of today and set in motion the future of our city.

Why these particular areas? Let's look at a common theme of today: economic development and the need to create jobs. Every politician wants to "create jobs." People need jobs, they say, but no job is created in isolation. Economic development cannot be just about creating jobs, but about creating the climate of attraction that makes people want to invest in your city. A job creator is much less likely to come into a city with inadequate schools, broken infrastructure, high crime, pollution, and a lack of worthwhile activities. Similarly, a person who lives in such a city will not find opportunities to advance.

And no detail is too small to ignore. The area around a giant building—the sidewalk, the bus benches, the garbage cans, the swales and medians—all coexist and contribute to the appearance of that building. If one element is missing, it strikes a discordant key. Think about flowers. If you plant flowers in a median, people are much less likely to litter. A clean median then leads to a clean neighborhood that leads to greater civic pride, lower crime, and the sense that people care about this place and want to live there. That creates attraction; economic opportunity follows.

Caring is also incredibly important—showing everyone that someone cares. I once asked former Chicago mayor Richard Daley what was the biggest issue he faced during his first election for mayor. He told me, abandoned cars. Imagine that! In Chicago, presently one of the most beautiful places in America and one of the greatest cities in the world, the mayor's main concern at the start of his term was abandoned cars. Yet abandoned cars littering the streets, much like trash, graffiti, pollution, broken sidewalks, or flooding—signals a lack of caring, a lack of pride.

If you don't care enough about your city or your neighborhood to clean it up, make it safe, get rid of that abandoned car, then why should anyone else? Job creators will move elsewhere. Opportunities for prosperity will go somewhere else. This is the reality we are missing in today's debate about the economy. Mayors understand this, which is why the economic engine of our nation is not found inside the Beltway or in our state capitals, but in our cities.

☐ ☐ ☐

GRAND IDEAS INSPIRE grand action. As I said before, when JFK said we were going to the moon, I am sure people around him scratched their heads and wondered, well, how are they going to manage that? But it ended up happening. I learned from JFK that part of being an effective leader is being a cheerleader. No matter whom I met, from a Fortune 500 CEO to a person at a coffee shop, I was always eager to share my idea for what Miami would become. I didn't care if anyone called me crazy or ambitious or grandiose; just by sheer positivity and belief I was willing to work harder than anyone to change people's minds. I always turned my words into action, and many of the projects you see in Miami today started with a handshake, a promise kept, and a bond of trust.

Others started to notice that I was excited about the potential that existed. People thought, well, if Manny sees this, if he is so excited about it, then there must be something to it. Little by little, the attitude of civic apathy was replaced with belief in the potential of Miami to become a great city. Even the bureaucrats started to buy in. Now everyone wanted to be part of the New Miami. We dreamed big, and others followed.

*Before leaving
Cuba. The party
may have been for
my fifth birthday,
my last in Cuba.*

Official team picture of Cuba Libre. I am number 13 (second row, standing).

With my mother and father after returning from the Bronco League World Series.

Law school graduation in June 1980 with my oldest son, six-year-old Manny, joining me. Today he is defensive coordinator of the University of Texas Longhorns.

Campaign brochure photo of my family in 2001. Standing: daughter Natalie, son Bobby, wife Robin, me, son Manny and his wife Stephanie. Seated: daughter Elisa, my mother Elisa, and first grandson Colin. Cinder is at Colin's feet.

I promised voters I would return, if elected mayor, to personally visit flooded streets. Here I am calling city staff for help with flooding. Ultimately, we installed a new pump station in this neighborhood, essentially eliminating the flooding problem.

City Hall goes green by installing solar panels to power the building.

At my family's first home— a rental apartment in Little Havana—during my first campaign for mayor.

Front of the mailer we sent to city residents for the kick-off event for Miami 21. 700 Miamians joined us that historic morning.

Artist's rendering of an aerial view of Museum Park.
In the foreground is the Patricia and Philip Frost
Museum of Science. To the rear is the Jorge M.
Pérez Art Museum. Both are located in Museum
Park in downtown Miami on Biscayne Bay.

View from Miami River looking east to the downtown
Miami skyline, with Marlins Park on the right.

Rendering of new Marlins ballpark, built on the site
of the former Orange Bowl in Little Havana. The
downtown skyline is in the background.

Gloating with New York City Mayor Michael Bloomberg and former New York City Mayor Rudy Giuliani after the Marlins defeated the Yankees at Yankee Stadium during the 2003 World Series.

Speaking at the 2008 Democratic National Convention in Denver.

With students at Holmes Elementary in Liberty City. We invested in after-school programming, encouraged significant parental involvement, and demolished the old school and built a new one.

Holding a press conference outside the White House as president of the U.S. Conference of Mayors. I and several other mayors had just met with newly elected President Barack Obama.

Chapter 8 Expanding Economic Opportunity

T HE LACK OF growth and investment in Miami led the city toward a decline where opportunities for prosperity and advancement were few. Miami, the headlines declared, was the poorest large city in America. The joke went that "moving on up" meant from fifth poorest to number one. As soon as I walked into City Hall, the press shoved a microphone in my face and expected me to deliver a ten-second solution to a problem that had developed over the past thirty to forty years. Poverty and lack of economic opportunity is not something that can be eradicated overnight, in five weeks, in five years, or even a decade. It would take time. Thus, I could not let the media or anyone else dictate my actions. I knew we had to address economic opportunity head on through a long-term strategic and comprehensive approach. No Miami mayor ever talked about poverty. They were afraid or in denial. But you can't solve a problem you refuse to admit exists. They also lacked a vision of how to address poverty. I began by admitting we had a problem. Then I set forth my grand idea—a climate of greater economic opportunity and prosperity. We announced a citywide Poverty Initiative, and for the first time ever, the city targeted funding specifically for poverty reduction. The results followed.

By the end of my eight years in office, we had developed a multifaceted approach known as ACCESS Miami. The ACCESS strategy would involve a municipal government in facilitating four basic principles: access to benefits, access to capital, accumulation of wealth and assets, and financial education leading to financial empowerment. This nationally recognized program became one of the nation's most comprehensive efforts to combat poverty. It recognized that not one single effort was enough, but various efforts, working in concert, were needed. Through a wide range of tools, including earned income and child care tax credits, small business support, micro lending, job placement and training, individual development accounts, savings and IRA accounts, and credit and financial education courses, we charted a course toward individual self-sufficiency—and a path to prosperity. ACCESS Miami has touched well over 100,000 people, putting hundreds of millions of dollars in the hands of those who need it most.

It all started when my policy director, Javier Fernández, came into my office and suggested that we start with the Earned Income Tax Credit (EITC)—a federal program designed to alleviate poverty. I had never heard of EITC, so Javier explained it to me. EITC had a proven track record in helping move five million people out of poverty every year. He continued with the program's merits and it became clear to me that this was a no-brainer. According to the IRS, we had a huge percentage of people in Miami who were failing to claim millions of dollars annually. This was compounded by the fact that we were a large immigrant population that had no idea this program existed and that they were entitled to these refunds.

I knew we needed EITC to be more than a one-time shot. I also knew we would need a full-blown public outreach campaign. In came my grassroots campaign experience. I held a press conference to announce our effort, and immediately our phones started ringing off the hook. We set up phone banks and prepared flyers and door hangers to explain the EITC. To save money, we used our solid waste department to distribute the flyers and door hangers. This was ideal since that department visits every home in Miami three times a week. We also polled city residents to verify IRS data about how many people were aware of the program and how many had actually ever claimed it. We also asked who prepared their tax returns. We learned that half our eligible residents were not claiming EITC. We also learned that traditional tax preparers—accountants, for example—were not the predominant tax preparers in low-income minority and immigrant communities. Tax preparation was done by nontraditional sources: private immigration offices, check cashing services, or notaries. In addition, paid tax preparers such as H&R Block and Jackson Hewitt prepare approximately 25 percent of all tax returns in the United States. Added to the other nontraditional sources, these are the largest group of tax preparers in America. Using information from city occupational licenses, we compiled a list of these tax preparers and sent them mailers letting them know about the EITC. Radio and television stations aired our message. Now we were reaching beyond City of Miami to the entire Miami media market. In the first year, we made at least 30,000 calls through our phone banks. We kept data on whom we called, and would call them in succeeding years reminding them to claim the EITC.

It also occurred to me that we could train city employees to prepare free tax returns. The city had thirteen outreach offices called Neighborhood Enforcement Teams (NET) throughout every neighborhood in the city. NET staff were trained to prepare tax returns. We installed computers to allow direct electronic filing. Our partners, the IRS, helped train our employees and opened free tax preparation sites on weekends and nonworking hours. Our NET employees would also be trained for our Benefit Bank program, discussed later in this chapter.

Claiming EITC meant that a low-income working individual could receive a substantial tax refund of up to $4,000–5,000 per year. If you had never claimed EITC before, you could also amend your prior years' tax returns, possibly tripling the amount of the refund. When I left office, over 80 percent of eligible Miamians were claiming EITC. I saw that EITC was putting money in people's pockets, so I turned to Javier and asked, how can we help them grow the pie? It was not enough to get people EITC refunds. We had to do more, and this is how we began to advance financial literacy.

The first question became: do you have a bank account? Many members of minority and immigrant communities do not. So we helped people set up bank accounts—a checking account, a savings account, an IRA. The idea was to connect the unbanked with financial institutions. In fact, the partnership with H&R Block, described later in this chapter, led to the establishment of over 5,000 checking, savings and retirement accounts in one tax season alone.

We also developed and implemented Individual Development Accounts (IDA). The City of Miami's Matched Savings Fund (MSF) is an example of a successful IDA program that leverages a resident's ability to save. The MSF is a federally and locally funded program designed to encourage persons of low income to accumulate assets. The MSF will provide a match equal to two dollars for each dollar an individual participant deposits into an MSF savings account (from earned income or from EITC, for example). This was a way for residents to start building up a nest egg for buying their first home, capitalizing a small business, or paying for postsecondary education. Home ownership improves neighborhoods and encourages small business creation. This expansion adds jobs. The city also increases its tax base. A two-for-one investment returns exponential dividends.

□ □ □

OUR MOVE TOWARD free income tax filing had a positive impact on private tax preparers like H&R Block and Jackson Hewitt. We found that low-income residents often used these companies because they offered rapid refund loans. To secure immediate access to refund money, the companies would advance all or a portion of the refund to the taxpayer. This was, of course, highly enticing to a person in need of immediate cash. However, the loans came at a very high cost, since the tax preparation companies would charge 25 or 30 percent interest on the advance. These were usurious rates—charged for money the taxpayers were entitled to. On the other hand, if you had a bank account, and filed electronically, the IRS could wire the money to your account in approximately ten days. But many people were motivated by the notion that "I need the money now, and I don't have any other way to receive it." By establishing bank accounts, they could realize the immediate benefit of not having to borrow their own money if they were willing to wait for the short time for the funds to be wired to their new bank account.

H&R Block and Jackson Hewitt learned of our program and asked if they could become part of our financial literacy campaign. The companies agreed to charge Miami residents a reduced rate to prepare tax returns, somewhere in the range of $25 to $50 per return during the first five years. More importantly, they also agreed to end the practice of rapid refund loans. Instead, they would partner with the city on our financial literacy program, working with customers to establish checking, savings, and retirement accounts, including Individual Retirement Accounts. As a result, utilizing the funds they had now set aside, dozens of our residents became homeowners for the first time. In fact, many of these were, in turn, referred to our own affordable housing program discussed later in this chapter.

With EITC, financial literacy, and IDAs all working, I wondered if there weren't additional programs and benefits people were not aware of. Logically, someone eligible for EITC must also be eligible for other benefits.

Miami was one of the first cities in the country to offer what we called the Benefit Bank: making it possible for residents to access, in one step, other government benefits they were entitled to but typically not receiving. Through an Internet-based platform, people had a simple, less time-consuming way to access food stamps, children's health insurance, Medicaid, energy bill assistance, federal income tax preparation, free application for federal student assistance (FAFSA), voter registration, and other assistance. Hundreds of millions of dollars were now made more readily available. For example, a single parent of two earning $15,000 a year could receive $4,824 in EITC, $453 additional Child Tax Credit, $3,089 in Children's Health Insurance, $3,469 in food stamps, and $200 in Low Income Home Energy Assistance, for a total of $12,030 in additional income, nearly doubling her or his income. We also used the Internet to create a job posting and training site where people could get information on matching their skills with available jobs. Accessmiamijobs.com now would receive over 40,000 unique visits per month.

□ □ □

SMALL BUSINESS IS the economic backbone of Miami and most other American cities.. These neighborhood job creators offer the greatest opportunity for economic advancement, especially in minority communities. We struck a first of its kind partnership with the Small Business Administration (SBA) to provide loans for our immigrant community. The SBA director came to Miami, and we executed a memorandum of understanding forming the basis for a national model later adopted by the U.S. Conference of Mayors for all cities in America. Hundreds of millions of dollars in SBA-backed loans were made available to small, minority businesses throughout Miami. Minority-owned businesses now had access to capital they would otherwise not have. This allowed them to expand and create new jobs.

We also launched a partnership with ACCION USA, an international micro-lender that had principally focused on Latin America and that chose Miami as its gateway to expand into the United States. These microloans—some as little as $500—provided capital for the smallest businesses. For example, the owner of a landscaping business who wanted to expand and needed to buy a new lawn mower could probably not walk into a large bank and secure a $500 loan. Through micro-lending, however, this was now possible.

The city itself awarded millions of dollars in contracts annually for a variety of services and products. Our efforts in this area increased the number of small, minority firms doing business with the city by over 100 percent. In cooperation with the U.S. Department of Commerce, we also opened a one-stop center to provide small business assistance with loan packages, procurement programs, and business management services.

In 2006, as part of the ongoing anti-poverty initiative, I brought before the City Commission a proposal for a living wage ordinance. A living wage recognizes the difference between the wage required to live in a particular locality and the federal minimum wage. Under the ordinance, which passed unanimously, city employees and those who work for certain contractors doing business with the city were to be paid a higher hourly wage (more than double the minimum wage) if the employer afforded the employee health insurance; if health insurance was not provided, an even higher hourly wage had to be paid. The federal minimum wage in 2006 was $5.15 per hour.

The anti-poverty and financial literacy programs that make up ACCESS Miami did not require much direct funding from the city. They took existing programs and made them accessible to residents of the city in order to allow them to find work and to build their own assets and wealth. We also capitalized on a strong public-private business synergy, drawing on partners such as the Mortgage Bankers Association, Consumer Credit Counseling Services, InCharge Education Foundation, Florida Jumpstart, Bank of America, H&R Block, and faith-based organizations.

□ □ □

THE EFFORT TO create prosperity had to include the faith-based community. It was president George W. Bush, a Republican, who promoted the idea of engaging churches and other faith leaders in social matters. The fact that mayors—most of whom are Democrats—were receptive to this notion goes back to the nonpartisan nature of mayors. When mayors see something they like and think can work in their city, they adopt it. It doesn't matter from which side of the aisle the idea originated; if it makes sense, use it.

Mayors had traditionally worked with faith-based organizations, such as the YMCA. If there was new incentive to further work with faith-based organizations for after-school programs or other community-based activities, then it made sense to expand these relationships. Our work with the faith-based community began with the effort to inform residents of the EITC. We asked religious leaders to help us get the word out. Places of worship now became an integral part of our efforts to attack poverty. Through our quarterly Pastoral Roundtable break-fasts, we developed an active, ongoing working partnership that proved useful in other circumstances where it was necessary to have a level of trust between government and religious leaders that wasn't centered on a crisis.

Most often, when there is a police shooting, for example, the typi-cal scene is one at which a member of the clergy holds a press conference, and asks for calm and God's help for the family. Then the politicians and police meet with the family and the clergy, hoping to defuse ten-sions. Everyone then goes home. This does not build trust. There isn't a real familiarity based on a working relationship. But now, because of the work of the city government and the faith-based communities, there is a partnership based on something other than a crisis.

This partnership helped me to form bonds with an incredibly diverse clergy. Miami's diversity of population brings with it diversity of worship, even within a specific ethnicity or race. This became clear when I served as a principal spokesman against the repeal of Miami's human rights ordinance, one that also protects sexual orientation. Evangelical Christians mounted a petition drive to repeal the ordinance, which I strongly opposed. Needless to say, at my next meeting with faith leaders, I had some very unhappy Evangelicals in the room. We clearly disagreed. In the past, an issue like this would have become personalized, political, polarizing, and difficult to resolve. But that didn't happen. I think part of the reason is that we knew each other. They appreciated the fact that we were working together in so many different ways to help the members of their churches. This partnership far outweighed our disagreement on one issue, no matter the emotions on both sides.

◻ ◻ ◻

ONE OF THE results of having a city where everyone wants to live is that property values and prices go up. It's simple economics: demand outpaces supply. Before I took office, no one wanted to live in Miami. We didn't have an affordable housing problem: everything was affordable. After I took office, that was no longer true. We wanted to attract new residents, but we also wanted to make sure that those who had stayed in the city would not be displaced.

Because of my background, making homeownership a greater possibility for people is a big deal for me. Remember that I come from a family that had to move every time the landlord raised the rent $25. The stability of having a roof over your head was a major priority for me. My policies reflected this concern.

When I arrived at City Hall, Miami's entire affordable housing portfolio consisted of three residential units with a total investment of under $400,000. Those numbers were astonishing. Part of the problem was that the city's affordable housing efforts relied on people who couldn't get the job done, who had no experience building anything.

Many were from community-based organizations that had projects awarded to them because of political connections to City Hall. When an affordable housing project was awarded, the city would transfer land to the development group, in many cases without a reverter clause, which would have allowed the city to reclaim the property had the development not taken place within a certain time. Some projects went as far back as the 1980s, with nothing built on the land. Because of the transfer and lack of reverter, the property was now in the hands of a private individual or organization, and the city couldn't get it back. In fact, in some cases, the developer actually sold the land for a profit.

To make the problem worse, the city had also committed millions of dollars to projects that it could not otherwise use since the money was tied up for those projects. This had to stop. We set out to reclaim as much of that property, recover as much of that money as we could. We had to demand repayment of past due loans—some transfers included city loans—and put the property and money back under city control. I then reached out to private sector affordable housing developers with a track record of actually completing projects. These developers expressed the same concerns voiced by their market rate colleagues; they simply did not trust the city. I convinced them that we had taken politics out of the system, and that we were serious about increasing our affordable and workforce housing production. An independent commercial loan housing review board, comprising citizens with expertise in housing development, would insulate projects from politics. This group would make the ultimate decisions on funding and awarding of projects. No longer did the City Commission award projects based on political considerations. We offered incentives such as deferred impact fees, a permit expediter at City Hall, and an ordinance to speed up foreclosures of abandoned lots and vacant buildings. Through our infill housing program, we made city-owned lots available for a dollar to those willing to build affordable and workforce housing.

With these tools in place, we set a goal of a billion dollars in affordable housing projects by the end of the decade—basically the end of my term. I wanted it to go from three units and a total investment of $380,000 to a billion dollars—grand ideas. We ended up exceeding our goal, with approximately $1.1 billion in total projects by the time I left office. The private sector responded, and we were able to leverage $10 for every dollar the city invested.

This is particularly noteworthy because two factors at play during this period presented real challenges. There was an incredible housing boom in America and certainly in Miami. This meant pricing people out of the market. But where were the people who worked for the city—the teachers, secretaries, police officers, and firefighters—going to live? They couldn't afford to live in Miami anymore. With the real estate boom expanding, available land became scarce, more valuable, and more expensive, thereby making construction more expensive. We faced a significant number of obstacles to creating a real affordable housing market. Still, we got the job done.

Through the years, the city had come to own a fairly significant number of parcels of land; most were vacant. Few things are worse for a neighborhood than a vacant lot because of all the things that empty space brings with it. I said we had to get rid of these lots. Our infill housing program "privatized" 98 percent of them. We needed to talk to developers and get them built. Miami also had an affordable housing trust fund. Developers would pay monies into the fund in exchange for greater density "bonuses" for their projects. Since there were no major projects being built, there was no money going into the fund. This all changed when greater development started to take place. Envisioning this would happen, we also substantially increased the amount developers had to contribute to the fund to get their bonus. As a result, in excess of $20 million was generated for affordable and workforce projects.

As if all these obstacles were not enough, our State Legislature proved of little help. Florida decided to fill budget holes using money that was originally supposed to go into a statewide affordable housing trust fund named after Bill Sadowski, a great public servant who met an untimely death, and was also a friend of mine. While the state and federal government were cutting funds we could have used to build affordable and workforce housing, the need continued, and we needed to figure out innovative ways to fill this gap. We also reached out beyond the traditional private sector affordable housing developers and made an effort to work with small business minority developers. In Liberty City, we partnered with a young entrepreneurial African American named Ario Lundy who had grown up in the neighborhood. If anyone knew what that neighborhood needed, it was Ario.

Ario went a step farther, answering my desire for green and environmentally friendly construction. One day he came to me and announced that his next two single family homes were going to be "green." I almost didn't believe him. But he returned with an architect and showed me a set of plans, and the two homes were ultimately Leadership in Energy and Environmental Design (LEED) certified. LEED was developed by the United States Green Building Council. It is a rating system that provides building owners and operators with a framework for identifying and implementing practical and measurable green building design, construction, operations, and maintenance solutions. These two homes became the first LEED certified, affordable single family homes in the state of Florida. Best of all, they were both in Miami's inner city.

▢ ▢ ▢

ONE OF THE greatest challenges to alleviating poverty in a city and expanding opportunities for prosperity is posed by the population of homeless. To me it was inhumane to round up homeless individuals and ship them somewhere else as some of our neighboring cities did. This was especially true when those cities were dropping off their homeless in our downtown! A people, a government must be judged by how it treats the most vulnerable among us. Given the complexity of the reasons for people becoming homeless, we had to adopt a comprehensive approach.

It began when we started working very closely with the Homeless Trust of Miami-Dade County, started by the late Alvah Chapman, former publisher of the *Miami Herald*. This unique countywide institution is funded by a 1 percent tax on restaurant meals. We are probably the only jurisdiction in America that taxes itself to help the homeless. We began placing homeless people into a continuum of care, a substantive effort to assist the homeless rather than simply moving someone off the streets temporarily for Chamber of Commerce purposes. This approach helps people get back on their feet. It also means helping someone find a job or moving them into permanent or transitional housing. We also helped with any health issues that prevented homeless people from becoming self-sufficient. Our continuum of care sought to identify the root cause of homelessness, provide a long term response, and move people off the streets and into a productive life.

In Miami, we saw an overall decrease of over 50 percent in our homeless population. We also reduced chronic homelessness by 30 percent. The chronic homeless—those who had substance abuse and mental problems—in many cases would resist being brought into shelters and incorporated into the continuum of care. They would rather continue to live on the streets. Any reduction of this population group was difficult.

In yet another effort to move our homeless into the continuum of care programs and services, we also had to address the issue of street feedings. Over the years, many well-meaning churches and individuals thought they would help the homeless population by providing sandwiches to individual homeless people on the streets. There were several problems with these good intentions. For one, it helped perpetuate homelessness. If you are on the street and know you will receive food each day, there is no incentive—especially among the chronically homeless—to try to do something else with yourself. It also created an enormous litter problem, with the Styrofoam boxes and cups used to deliver the food ending up on our streets. We worked with churches and other institutions and convinced them that a better solution to feeding the homeless is to bring them into shelters. There they can have a decent meal sitting at a table rather than on a sidewalk. In addition, the shelters have bathrooms, allowing people to use the facilities for cleaning up. The shelter also took care of the litter problem. We found this approach very effective in luring people off the streets and persuading them to accept placement in the continuum of care. We also started a program called Miami Cares, modeled after one that former mayor of San Francisco Gavin Newsom (to become 49th lieutenant governor of California) had started in San Francisco. Our homeless outreach program was staffed almost 100 percent by formerly homeless individuals. In many cases, these workers knew the current homeless people by name and knew where to find them. These people had been on the street themselves. Under Miami Cares, we brought the homeless into a single location. There they could take a shower, shave, and phone their family. We would facilitate such phone calls, even if long distance. If they had family in other parts of the country and wanted to return home, we would arrange transportation for them. We had hundreds of homeless people show up at our locations, and none of this would have been possible without the help of thousands of volunteers who helped make Miami Cares a resounding success.

Another aspect of our work with the homeless centered on a homeless shelter in downtown Miami called Camillus House. Originally established to help Cuban refugees in the 1960s by the Little Brothers of the Good Shepherd, a Catholic religious order, Camillus House had through time transitioned to become a homeless shelter. The original facility is in downtown Miami, and is one of the reasons the homeless population concentrated in that area.

Camillus House offers a meal program for the homeless, so that population would spend the day in the area waiting for the distribution of the day's meal. The facility itself was old and falling apart, too small to accommodate the number of homeless who wanted to make use of its programs. Since the 1980s there had been ongoing debates and arguments about moving Camillus House out of downtown Miami. Everyone was aware that the facility had an important role to play, but its location and condition meant it also dampened any efforts to revitalize the area. Camillus House itself was anxious to move, realizing that its facility was worn and obsolete. Of course, this discussion led to the NIMBY issue—not in my backyard. No one wanted a homeless shelter in their neighborhood.

Despite decades of opposition and inaction, I committed myself to finding Camillus House a new home that would be worthy of the great work done for so many years. We identified a potential large site (outside downtown) in the area around Jackson Memorial Hospital/University of Miami Medical School. The State of Florida no longer needed an old right of way parcel abutting Interstate 95. Coincidentally, the university owned a smaller site immediately south of the larger site. Properties abandoned by one state agency are first offered to other state agencies. In fact, this large parcel had been requested and committed to another state agency. We would need to convince the state to reverse this decision.

Years earlier, Donna Shalala, president of the University of Miami—former Health and Human Services secretary in the Clinton administration—and I had formed the Miami Partnership, modeled after the one former Philadelphia mayor Ed Rendell and University of Pennsylvania president Judith Rodin had created to revitalize the university district in West Philadelphia. Although the university and the city were the principal partners, the Miami Partnership would also include numerous public and private institutions in the area. Local economic development officers devote a great deal of time and resources to recruit businesses into their respective cities. They pat themselves on the back when they recruit a widget manufacturing plant with twenty-two employees to their city. I disagree with this approach. Why not first look in your own backyard? For example, this area has over 30,000 employees and receives 50,000 visitors daily. Why not build and expand your existing economic engines?

The Miami Partnership rebranded this area, formerly known as the Civic Center area, now calling it the Health District. The University would make a significant investment with a goal of building a major research institution in the area with millions of square feet of bio-science facilities. In turn, the city would invest in numerous infrastructure projects, including a new public transit trolley system, and would create zoning to accommodate the University's plans.

It was a complicated plan. Besides convincing the state to reverse its prior decision and arrange to have Camillus House control the large site, we would then need to orchestrate a land swap between the University and Camillus House. The completed deal would have the University controlling the larger site and Camillus controlling the smaller property previously owned by the University. The new site was the perfect place for Camillus House. The University would obtain a parcel of land large enough to house its proposed project. The University and Camillus House would also benefit from their close proximity, allowing them to collaborate on projects to help the homeless. Governor Jeb Bush, President Shalala, and Dr. Paul Ahr, president of Camillus House, made this complicated deal possible.

Only one issue remained: convincing the district commissioner for the area, Angel González, to support yet another homeless shelter in his district. When I first advised him of the plan, he was very unhappy. As with so many other areas of the city, the district he represented and the neighborhood where the new facility would be sited, Allapattah, had been long neglected. The area had been allowed to decay from lack of public and private investment. To make matters worse, governments at all levels had dumped halfway houses, other homeless shelters, and other facilities no one wanted in their neighborhoods into the area.

Elected with me in 2001, Commissioner Gonzalez had created a climate of public and private investment. In fact, his district had seen more private investment than any other area of Miami outside the downtown area. Naturally, he and a lot of his constituents were not happy we were contemplating this site for yet another homeless facility. After many years and numerous public and private meetings, Gonzalez and his constituents accepted the plan. Chief among the reasons they accepted included the fact that the University, not Camillus House, would control the larger site on the northern end of the land assemblage. The north parcel served as the district boundary and would be a buffer to Camillus House.

Equally important was the fact that the city imposed (and Camillus accepted) numerous restrictions on the new facility that addressed many of the concerns of Commissioner Gonzalez, including a curfew, no street feeding, availability of rehabilitative and treatment services, security, landscape buffers, and other conditions to internalize the operation (inside not outside the facility) and serve only Camillus clients. None of us wanted to replicate the old facility in downtown Miami at the new site, and these and other conditions adequately addressed the failures of the downtown site. Finally, UM's new biosciences facility is estimated to create 5,000 good paying jobs. The obvious positive economic impact to the area continues to be a very compelling reason. After more than twenty years of debate over this very emotional and polarizing issue, the new Camillus House opened in 2011. It could not have happened without the leadership and vision of Commissioner Gonzalez.

The director of President Bush's Interagency Council on Homelessness, Phil Mangano, visited Miami several times to observe our various efforts on behalf of the homeless. Miami received an award from this agency, making me among a handful of mayors in the country to be recognized for their work on homelessness. Phil always told me: "We hate homelessness, but we love the homeless." This sentiment was carried throughout our efforts, and in the end many individuals and families were given new opportunities because of it.

　　▢　▢　▢

　　RELIANCE ON FAITH-BASED organizations and partnerships with private businesses, job creation, ACCESS Miami, workforce development, small business assistance and micro-lending, the Benefit Bank, EITC, financial literacy programs, making sure homeownership was accessible, caring for our homeless, and other initiatives were all parts working together toward a grand idea—creating opportunities for people to pull themselves and their families out of poverty. Many of our initiatives have become models for other cities. Miami was even among the original members of the Cities for Financial Empowerment Coalition, devoted to developing national financial empowerment programs.

　　Today, Miami is no longer the poorest major city in America. Our fight against poverty would necessarily include one additional critical component: education.

Chapter 9 Education

I AM AN EXAMPLE of someone who beat poverty through education. Without access to a good education, who knows where I'd be now? It is therefore impossible for me to conceive of any kind of strategy that provides opportunities for advancement out of poverty that does not make improving education the top priority.

Because of the way school districts operate in America, most mayors have no control over schools. We have no say over the most important determinative factor that impacts the future course of our city. Miami has a separate, independent school board, with taxing authority, charged with operating the public schools. No prior mayor had ever sought to challenge this authority. If city schools were underperforming and neglected, it was easier to claim that it was not the mayor's fault and blame others instead.

While mayors are well known to most residents of a city, the same cannot be said of school board members. The media and the voters pay much more attention to city government than they do to the governance of those entrusted with our children's future. Historically, this has created a lack of accountability on the part of the school board. If the school system isn't doing its job and the mayor is in charge, you know where to find the mayor. Typically, school board members receive attention only during election time or when a scandal breaks.

Inspired by mayors such as Richard Daley in Chicago and Michael Bloomberg in New York, who took control of their school systems, I thought the mayor of Miami should take control of the city schools. I welcomed that accountability and began the process. The idea was that I would be responsible for running the schools, with the school board chair and the school system superintendent answering to me. Shortly after I was elected, I went to our state capital and had a bill filed that would have transferred control over city schools to the city. The bill passed the Florida House of Representatives, but we didn't have enough time to get it passed through the Florida Senate. Before I could get to the next legislative session, two positive developments occurred.

At the end of 2002, elections were held for the Miami-Dade County School Board and I threw my support behind several candidates. Some people who had been on the board for a while were replaced with people who shared my passion for the children of Miami. That was the first important change. The second change resulted from the hiring of a new school superintendent. I made sure I was on the superintendent selection committee. If I could not take over the schools right away, the next best thing was to put someone in charge I could trust and work with, someone who cared deeply about children and who would fight along with me for education equality—more important, someone who understood my frustration with the way schools were run in Miami.

The two finalists for the job were Rudy Crew, former chancellor of the New York school system, and the Cuban American superintendent of the Nashville school system. The politically expedient thing would have been to vote for my fellow Cuban American. Instead, I recommended Crew because I thought he was the best man for the job. In the end, Crew was selected.

Rudy knew I was interested in taking over the school system. I had been very direct in telling him so. He told me he understood my frustrations, and was well aware of the national trend of mayors wanting to take over their schools. Rudy asked that I give him a chance. He promised to work with me. So I sat back, thought about it, and agreed. We had a new school board and a new superintendent. That meant we had a fresh opportunity to do something positive. Rudy and I shook hands and pledged to work together. Still, I wanted something in writing that would formalize our relationship.

I had hired two teachers, Lisa Martinez and Vivianne Bohorques, to work with me in the Mayor's Office. This was something completely new as these positions had not existed in my predecessor's organizational chart. Prior to Crew's arrival, Lisa led our efforts to establish a mentoring initiative targeted at our F-rated elementary school, obtained a five-year $3.5 million Twenty-First Century grant from the U.S. Department of Educationfor this school to address out-of-school programming needs, established a Miami Youth Council, and secured funding from the Children's Trust for out-of-school programming at our city parks focused on literacy and enrichment activities.

Miami is one of the few jurisdictions that taxes itself to support children's programs. Thanks to the outstanding leadership of Dave Lawrence, Jr. (a former *Miami Herald* publisher), Miami-Dade voters in September 2002 approved an independent special district, a dedicated funding source for children. The vote was 2–1 in favor. A "sunset provision" required that the initiative be returned within five years for voter approval. That vote took place in August 2008. Despite the difficult economic climate, Miami-Dade voters approved the reauthorization of the Trust, this time by an overwhelming 86 percent. The Children's Trust proved to be an invaluable resource. Without this dedicated source of funding, we would not have been able to implement a significant portion of our educational initiatives. I campaigned in support of the measure in 2002 and 2008, and I am proud to live in a community willing to invest in its children.

Shortly after Crew's arrival, Lisa, Vivianne, and I began to work with his staff, led by Crew's second in command, Alberto Carvalho. Alberto would succeed Crew as our superintendent. He has become a highly respected national leader in education, and, in my opinion, one of the best superintendents in America. Together, we developed the blueprint for a work plan that would define this new partnership. We called our plan the Education Compact and believe it to be the first of its kind in any major city. The Compact focused on three principal areas: student achievement, capital investment, and parental, community, and civic engagement. It also included very specific, measurable goals and action steps. I wanted to make sure that we had a clear and defined set of priorities, that we all knew what was expected of each other, and that we would be held accountable for getting there.

I also wanted the City Commission and School Board to approve the Compact, formalizing a relationship between the two entities for the first time in Miami history. This way, everyone had a stake in the outcome. The school superintendent would appear before the City Commission and report on progress, face questions, and respond to concerns from the city commissioners. The commissioners could now focus on their schools, become their advocates, and have their questions and concerns addressed directly on a regular basis by the superintendent. I, in turn, regularly appeared before the School Board, where the same process was followed.

There were measures the School Board could take that the city could not, and vice versa. The problem was that they were addressed in isolation. Now that they were working as a unit, the city was able to complement and enhance the Board efforts as active participants in the educational process. For example, because of funding cuts, many schools had to eliminate after-school and summer programs. On the other hand, our parks were open after school and during the summer. They had become a place where children could play, learn, and explore the arts. Now, children could go from school to our parks and play sports or receive tutoring, often from teachers paid with grants we secured. We also encouraged city employees to mentor students, giving them an hour of paid leave weekly to do so. The city and school board were finally working together.

◻ ◻ ◻

THE RESULTS FROM the Compact were extraordinary. By the end of my term, student achievement in the city of Miami had improved dramatically. According to the Florida Comprehensive Assessment Test (FCAT), which assigns grades to schools based on students' results on the test, when I took office only 10 percent of our schools were A or B, 63 percent were D or F, and our system-wide average was D. Today, almost 60 percent are A or B (with more A schools than any other grade), only 15 percent are D or F, and our system-wide average is B. The overall increase in student achievement and school performance should not overshadow the increases in grade-level proficiencies in math and English in schools that had traditionally underperformed. The long-term pattern is very positive. We had no more F elementary schools. Of 18,000 high schools nationally, 3 of ours are ranked in the top 100. Our school system was a finalist on several occasions for the prestigious Broad Award, and Rudy Crew was named National Superintendent of the Year by the American Association of School Administrators in 2008.

On the capital side, the School Board committed a half-billion dollars to improve city school facilities. This was an important shift since most of the capital funds had gone to suburban schools, leaving the city behind. The flight to suburbia of prior decades, and the resources which followed, had robbed city schools of vital capital improvements, especially those in the inner city. It was highly disturbing to walk into many of Miami's schools to find that they looked much like they did when I attended elementary school: cracked paint, broken windows, bathrooms that did not work, and the list goes on. How can we expect our children to learn, or care to learn, in an environment like this? I suppose their parents had given up too. Now, they had an advocate, their city government. We reversed this decline in school spending.

With the increased funding from the School Board, we rebuilt several schools and built three new high schools—an achievement particularly important to me because new families moving into the city would result in an increase in our school-aged population. As in most states in America, our schools are funded by a combination of state and local sources. Regrettably, our legislature has abdicated its responsibility to adequately fund education, instead choosing to push the funding obligation down to local taxpayers. This shell game allows state legislators to claim they "lowered taxes," and since the need still exists, the obligation is necessarily absorbed by local taxpayers. In fact, the percentage of the state's contribution to the total school budget has decreased, meaning that contributions at the local level have naturally increased. School boards have to raise taxes, so they become the bad guys. It is revolting when I listen to state leaders talk about job creation on the one hand, while they severely cut education funding on the other hand.

Rudy and I targeted a number of projects that we could jointly develop. He told me that he had created a young women's academy when he was New York City school chancellor and it had done very well. Today, in Miami, you will find both a Young Women's and a Young Men's Preparatory Academy, allowing parents to choose a public, single-gender college preparatory school for their children. Both have done extremely well and are A-rated. We also discussed developing academies in other specific areas: law enforcement, finance, and banking. The academies would be designed so that a student would not only take the required courses and electives needed to graduate, but also "major" in the school's target area. Students are more excited and energetic when they are focusing on something they like, even if it means taking the extra courses. They also benefit from the exposure of private sector lecturers who supplement the classroom teachers. This has led to higher student achievement in the academies.

Our discussion turned to the need for a training facility for the police department. We did not have one, but the city's 2001 general obligation bond set aside $10 million for such a facility. As with many of the line items included in the bond issue, there was no real connection between the amount approved and the actual construction cost of such a facility. When we started to focus on the design for a police training facility, it became clear that we did not have enough funding. I turned to my chief of police, John Timoney, to discuss our options. The chief had worked on a similar idea while in New York. He suggested we speak to Rudy about a possible joint venture. Interestingly, Chief Timoney and Rudy had known each other from their years in New York.

Rudy, John, and I met on several occasions to discuss the possibility of developing an academy for law enforcement that would focus on several areas, including law and forensic studies. We executed a joint development agreement which called on both parties to contribute funds based on their pro rata use of the facility now estimated to cost closer to $30 million. The city found the additional funds it was required to contribute, and the School Board continued to invest in city schools. We would design and build a facility (in downtown Miami, on city-owned land and located right next to our police department headquarters) that would serve as a police training facility and a high school with a special area of focus in law enforcement, forensic science, and homeland security. We were correct in our assumption that a school like this would generate a great deal of excitement.

With forensic science as the high school focus, students would not only be taught in a classroom setting, but then walk down a hallway and work with the real CSI Miami on investigations involving real-life cases. The high school is the first of its kind in the world, not because it is a criminal justice high school—there are few of them—but because it was embraced by the Police Department. The notion of police officers mixing with high school students can't be overstated. The academy opened shortly before I left office and is an A-rated school.

◻ ◻ ◻

WITH THE GOAL of encouraging students to become involved in public service, the Compact served to enhance our efforts through the Youth Council. Students from each of our high schools worked on projects during the school year that they selected based on the particular interests of their school. One high school had an alley behind it where a lot of illegal dumping was occurring. The alley was also rife with criminal activities, including drug dealing. The students' project was to come up with a solution to the issue they identified. They would work through the problem and then make a presentation to the city commissioners and me. Other projects included everything from teenage pregnancy to drug use to ethnic and racial relations.

Students would also be responsible for running a mock city commission meeting. They would take on the roles of mayor, city commissioners, and city manager. They would hold the meeting and make budget decisions on where to spend the city's money: parks or law enforcement. Students acting as department directors would have to make their case for funding their priorities. After the meeting, the city commissioners and I would provide them feedback. This was an invaluable experience for our high school students, allowing them to learn about their local government alongside our city's leaders.

Parental involvement was the third goal of the Compact and we achieved this goal primarily through the Parent Academy. Prior to the formation of the Parent Academy, we had established a Families First Parent Academy. Funded by the Children's Trust, it was directed at families with children up to five years old, helping prepare them prior to entering our school system. The Families First Parent Academy would later serve to complement the parental engagement efforts of the Parent

Academy. The Parent Academy exposed parents to their child's education, showing them what was happening in the classroom, fully engaging them in the education process. Having an involved parent plays a critical role in student performance. Parent Academy sessions were held on Saturdays in city parks so that the School Board didn't have to open a school on a weekend.

From our end, we linked the Parent Academy with ACCESS Miami. Not only were we able to help parents become more involved with their children's education, but also provided them with classes on basic banking practices, personal credit, homeownership, credit management, managing money, saving and investing. We had a captive audience: "As long as you're here learning about your child's progress, let's help you out too. Let's look at these benefit programs. Let's get you on a computer. Do you know how to use a computer? Do you have a job? Are you unemployed? Let's sit down and look for job opportunities. Fill out a job application. Help prepare a resume." We were able to connect many parents to the various elements of ACCESS Miami. The response was enthusiastic. Well over 100,000 parents went through the Parent Academy sessions and ACCESS Miami.

▢ ▢ ▢

THE SYNERGIES THAT occurred with the Parent Academy led us to create a way technology could be used to advance opportunities for the entire family. Elevate Miami—a nationally recognized partnership of the city, School Board, private sector, and philanthropy—uses technology to open up a new world of learning. The program touched the lives of thousands of Miamians, including seniors and low-income residents, by turning libraries, parks, and community and government centers into free access points to the world. This was especially important for our city's children.

As part of the Compact, our school partners developed the Rites of Passage curriculum. Every sixth grader in Miami who did well in school, followed the rules, and earned the respect of peers and adults had the opportunity to take home a free computer with free Internet access. Rites of Passage taught students more about the important skills in life that would lead to success, from shaking hands to looking someone in the eye, and even finding their way around Miami.

The last point is important. A significant number of children, especially those living in the inner city, had never been to the beach or other parts of Miami. Learning to use a map to get around is not only an essential life skill, but a way to broaden horizons. Parents were also required to participate by attending Parent Academy sessions focused on digital literacy, including Internet safety, to ensure that the family was prepared to bring technology into the home. Families who successfully completed all the requirements received a free computer to take home and free or reduced Internet access, so that child and household were connected to the world.

Deciding to make these investments was really quite simple: without them, the jobs and opportunities of the future will go elsewhere. The cycle of poverty would continue. And we as leaders would have failed our children and our city.

▫ ▫ ▫

MAYORS NEED CONTROL over education, whether directly or indirectly. At the very least, they need to become active participants in the education of their city's children. It is much too important, and directly impacts everything else in a city; every part of a mayor's agenda. The traditional "it's not my job" or "blame the school board" approach does not work anymore. If we are trying to create and maintain a sustainable city, if we are trying to fight crime, if we are trying to provide economic opportunity for residents, we need to improve the quality of education. For cities to remain competitive in the global marketplace, we must educate our children; if not, we will all lose. Furthermore, it is downright criminal to abandon these children without any real opportunity for a future.

How then can mayors not do something about education? These are our children. It's not as if they are living in some independent world controlled by a school board. These kids all live in Miami, in the neighborhoods of my city. I have to assume a responsibility for them, be their advocate. This is what makes sense. One of the first questions a Fortune 500 CEO asks when considering whether to locate in a city is, "How are your schools?" It is also the same question a young family asks thinking about moving back into the city from the suburbs. As the quality of its schools goes, so does the current and future state of a city.

In Miami, I was the first mayor to become involved in improving the condition of our schools, and our city and children are better off for it. Our graduation rates continue to increase, especially among minority students and our grade proficiencies continue to increase. As a result, we now outperform other school districts in Florida as well as comparable sized districts in the United States. As with the arts (see Chapter 13), Miami's growth had been stymied by an educational system not conducive to building a sustainable city. We changed that. While we were not successful in achieving control of city schools, we did the next best thing: we developed a true partnership with our school system and held them accountable for our children's education. It has worked.

Chapter 10 Making Neighborhoods Safe

THE MOST FUNDAMENTAL responsibility of government is to provide for the safety and security of its people. Successful policing involves more than just crime statistics; you must earn the trust of all residents through professionally trained police officers governed by a clear set of rules, including the use of force that respects the dignity and rights of your residents. It must also take into account improving the overall quality of life of a neighborhood. Catching bad guys is one thing, but making sure streets are clean, cracking down on illegal housing units and abandoned cars, even ridding the streets of roosters, all come together to make a place safe.

Like most major American cities during the late 1990s, Miami saw a significant reduction in crime. In spite of this progress, there existed a tremendous lack of confidence and anger toward the Police Department. In a city where the general population was already inherently cautious and distrustful of police (blacks due to civil rights issues and police behavior during riots; Cubans due to police being seen as an arm of dictatorial power), the police force had seemingly gone out of its way to widen this gulf of trust.

Miami's Police Department had become a symbol of everything

that could go wrong in policing. Questionable police shootings and cover-ups had led to several inner city riots (including the infamous McDuffie riots in the early 1980s, with over $100 million in damage). Officers were indicted and arrested for everything from running drugs and plotting murders (Miami River Cops) to beating suspects to death and planting evidence (Cano Mercado). The department also operated as an entity unto itself, becoming highly politicized and separate from the structure of City Hall. There were even allegations that police kept "secret files" on activities of politicians, causing some elected leaders to be afraid of questioning police action. Politicians also used police to intimidate their opposition. It became an incestuous relationship. Ultimately, prior to my election, the Miami Police Department had lost its certification from the Commission on Accreditation for Law Enforcement (CALEA), the national police rating agency.

The people of Miami spoke loud and clear at the ballot box. On the same ballot on which I was elected, over 70 percent of Miami voters approved creation of a Civilian Oversight Panel to monitor police activity and hold the department accountable for a wide variety of actions, from shootings to rude behavior during a traffic stop. All this served to perpetuate the perception that Miami was still a very unsafe city. If I wanted to lure people and investment back to Miami, all this had to change, and it started at the top.

◻ ◻ ◻

WHETHER RIGHT OR wrong, I shared with the people of Miami a complete lack of confidence in our police department. Shortly after my election, I invited the U.S. Department of Justice to conduct a thorough investigation of our police department's practices and procedures. I wanted to get to the bottom of what was happening, and I knew that I could not trust an internal investigation; the people who were causing the problems could not be trusted to fix them. The review of an independent law enforcement agency would give us a guide where to begin reforms.

Next, I was convinced that we needed to look for a new police chief. I had no confidence in the incumbent chief's ability to lead and reform the department. It became clear to me that numerous cliques had formed within the department. Prior mayors had sided with one clique to the exclusion of others. There was no loyalty in the department to the leadership, only to the clique. If you chose the chief from one group, the other groups would make it a point to work against him so their guy could become chief. This was not a meritocracy. If you were a political ally of the mayor, you became chief. Everyone else was demoted and went on the midnight shift.

I had to look outside the department for new leadership. One of the many odd things about Miami government is that the mayor does not get to hire the police chief; this duty rests with the city manager. When safety is your paramount responsibility, it is essential that the person entrusted with this, the police chief, have a very close personal and professional relationship with the mayor. To me, the chief of police is the most important position in Miami, or in any city.

I wanted to search nationally for a new chief because our residents and our department deserved the very best police chief we could find. During our search, City Manager Carlos Giménez would bring candidate after candidate to my office to say hello, so we could talk for a few minutes. After I compiled a short list, no one impressed me. With the challenges we were facing, I wanted a chief who was up to the task. I said to Carlos, "Is this the best we can do? Is this it? Are you satisfied with the applicants?" The answer came back, "No."

"Then perhaps you should keep working on this. We should not settle. We should strive to hire the best."

At the same time, a friend of mine had been talking to the police chief of a small municipality in Miami-Dade County. Somehow he was tapped into the national network of police chiefs and knew who was available. I asked him to provide us with a list of the top five police chiefs in America. He gave us a list with five names. It was a great list with prominent former or current chiefs of police from throughout the nation. Now we knew who the best were. The problem was that some had just started jobs in other cities or were unlikely to come to Miami because of life circumstances (for example, William Bratton, who had been police commissioner in New York, had just been hired as chief of police in Los Angeles, so he was unlikely to move a month later to Miami).

So, I asked, "What about John Timoney?" The former number two in the New York City Police Department and former Philadelphia commissioner was not currently employed as a chief of police. I was told Timoney was in a plush office in Manhattan at a high paying job with a security firm, wearing a nice suit and tie to work every day. My staff concluded it was unlikely he would come to Miami, especially since he would have to take a significant pay cut to run a department with a less than stellar reputation in a city he had never been to. I said, "There's only one way to find out for sure. Pick up the phone and call him."

Fortunately, John agreed to fly down to meet with me. He later confessed that he really had zero interest in the job, but came down to get a few days of sunshine during the bitter cold winter months in New York.

After he met with the city manager, Timoney wanted to meet with me. He came from cities (New York and Philadelphia) where the chief reported to the mayor, so he wanted to understand my vision for Miami and my commitment to public safety. Most important, he wanted to make sure that if he took the job, he could do so without political interference.

John and I sat outside on my terrace overlooking the bay and talked for a long time that evening. Knowing he was an avid rower, I purposely sat with my back to the bay. He could have a clear view of the unfrozen water behind me where he could envision himself rowing year round. I asked him point blank why he would even consider coming to Miami. "You've had a great career. You have a nice job now, making decent money. Why would you give all that up, put on a uniform again, and be out in the middle of the street at three in the morning after a shooting?"

He said, "Because I'm a cop. I miss it."

That impressed me greatly. You could just tell it was in his blood. It wasn't a job. He loved policing. He loved his cops.

John had risen through the ranks of one of the largest police departments in the world, going from beat cop to top cop, the youngest four star chief in NYPD history. It was Bratton, Jack Maple (who came up with COMPSTAT as a tool to track crime and measure police accountability), and Timoney who deserve the real credit for the reduction of crime in New York in the 1990s. John's educational background was also impressive. Generally, it is difficult to find a police chief with two master's degrees, in Urban Planning and in American History.

As though all this were not enough, what impressed me the most about Timoney was his civil libertarian bent. There would be instances later when I would lose patience with a sequence of events, and it was the chief who was much more inclined than I was to urge restraint in using the power of government. I would say, "Damn it, we should do this" and he would respond, "No, we can't."

After our meeting, Timoney took the job. Controversy soon followed. The incumbent police chief was Cuban American. Many thought that his replacement must also be Cuban American. In fact, commissioner Angel Gonzalez took to the airwaves in order to criticize my decision. It would be the only time during the eight years he and I served together that an issue divided us so strongly. Obviously, the police union and others wanted one of their own, from inside the department. Finally, a number of black clergy had urged me to consider a black candidate. My response was uniform; the issue is not ethnicity, race, or parochialism. Miami deserves the best chief of police, and we succeeded in finding him. John Timoney's impressive character was reflected in how he managed the police department: how he handled the men and women; how he developed a model use of force policy; and how he earned the trust of those in every community in Miami.

□ □ □

ON THE DAY Timoney was sworn in as police chief, nearly a dozen City of Miami police officers were standing federal trial for controversial police shootings. Miami had a history of questionable police shootings, some leading to riots in the 1980s and 1990s. This helped fuel a perception in the community that the police were trigger happy, with a "shoot first, ask questions later" mentality. So I asked how all this helped achieve my goal of building a sustainable city, of encouraging people who had abandoned city life to move back: no arts, a poor educational system, and an unsafe city with a police department that could not be trusted.

Chief Timoney began his reform of the police department by implementing the most progressive use of force policy in the United States. Officers were now expected to use force as their last resort, after having exhausted all other options. The chief explained to me that this was good not only for the community, but for cops too, since the last thing you want is to find yourself suspended or on trial for shooting someone.

During a SWAT raid around Christmas, 2003, an armed criminal had barricaded himself in a house to avoid arrest and fired shots at our officers. The SWAT commander, lieutenant Armando Guzman (coincidentally, an old Belen school friend), called in, and Timoney asked if the gunman was aware of the ongoing police record of not discharging their weapons. Lieutenant Guzman replied that while the gunman might not be aware of the no shoot record, he and his officers certainly were, and would do their best to keep the record going. SWAT held fire, and eventually the gunman was talked out of the house. So it happened: not a single shot, and the criminal eventually gave up. This example helps illustrate the point that police officers will almost always react in accordance with the clear message articulated at the top. It is the chief of police and the mayor who are responsible for conveying that message.

If use of force, especially deadly force, is required to protect an officer's life or that of a civilian, an officer should respond accordingly. However, if a gunman is barricaded inside a building, the response need not always follow the typical shootout popularized by Hollywood in cops and robbers movies or John Wayne westerns. Shooting at a moving car is yet another area where restraint is at issue. Officers who stand directly in front of high-speed automobiles have placed themselves in a situation in which firing at the car is their only resort. But why stand in front of the car in the first place? Why put yourself in a position where your only resort is to fire at the car? Indeed, firing at a moving car will very often lead to the fatal shooting or serious injury of innocent bystanders.

The use of force policy significantly reduced the number of police shootings to the point where our department went twenty consecutive months, from the moment Timoney was sworn in, without a single officer firing his or her weapon, all while increasing arrests and reducing crime. This was later repeated for additional twelve- and ten-month periods. That's historically unheard of in big city policing.

Our use of force policy also required that our police officers undergo training on how to deal with mentally ill persons. Many shootings throughout the country have resulted from a failure of police to recognize the mental instability and challenges of the person they encountered. Our Crisis Intervention Team became a national model for dealing with the mentally disabled. As a result, our police had thousands of encounters with mentally disabled persons all without incident.

Chief Timoney rewrote most if not all the policies and procedures for the department, from use of force to how police officers dress. He also emphasized training—sending police officers to the FBI Academy in Quantico, Virginia, for example—along with just getting the department better educated, using new technologies and tactics: everything was all about giving the men and women on the force the tools they needed to be better police officers and stay out of trouble. Miami's police department instituted sweeping changes, including reengineering the Internal Affairs department to be more proactive while no longer located in central headquarters, implementing a new system of discipline with clear rules and an early warning system for violations, videotaping confessions of suspects, reintroduction of random drug testing of officers, strengthening property and inspection units, even changing the way shootings were investigated.

John brought his own personal experience but also worked on building the expertise and the knowledge of his team so they could do a better job. His staff, led by deputy chief Frank Fernandez, made a huge difference for Miami, restoring the reputation of our department and the trust of our residents. After completing the review I requested, the Department of Justice gave our police department a clean bill of health based on our reforms, the first city ever to receive such recognition. The department also regained its CALEA certification in late 2005/early 2006, the first available certification period during Chief Timoney's tenure.

WHEN I INITIALLY spoke with John, I told him I couldn't do all the things I wanted to do—bring back investment, reenergize the city, and convince people to move back into Miami—unless he did his job. If there was a perception that it is not safe to live in the city, people would not invest, not build new housing, and not return. The police department would be key in determining whether the city could get out of its slump.

Soon, John Timoney was everywhere. An urban lore had developed in other cities where John had worked: chasing down criminals on foot, stopping purse snatchings and muggings, and many other stories. A mere glance from John's Irish face could freeze bad guys. He was in the neighborhoods, going into the churches, meeting with community groups, riding his bike up and down city streets. Just as he had done in New York City and Philadelphia, in Miami he also personally ran down, tackled, and arrested a purse snatcher.

Chief Timoney would often say to me, "Mr. Mayor, there's going to come a point where you can't reduce the crime rate any more. For example, there's only so much you can do about domestic shootings. If a husband and wife want to shoot each other, there's nothing we can do about it. We can't be inside the house. At a certain level, you're just going to have crime. Period. Don't think that every year we're going to have these drops." Still, the crime rate dropped dramatically, and Miami's crime rate lowered to 1960 levels in all categories and all neighborhoods. For example, consider homicides. In 1980 and 1981, Miami had its highest number of homicides, 220. By comparison, New York City had its highest number of homicides, 2,245, in 1990. During the two worst years in the history of these cities, if Miami's population had equaled that of New York City in 1980 and 1981, its total homicides would have approximated 5,000 during those years, more than twice the number in New York City during its worst year in history. During my term, we had two years in which our total homicides fell below 60. This was a 76 percent decline in homicides from our record year and matches the decline experienced by New York City from the bad days of 1990.

As the crime rate came down, people felt that they could walk their dog in the middle of the night, go jogging, and take their kids to parks reclaimed from criminals. The police were protecting citizens and conducting themselves professionally. They were there to help. Chief

Timoney became famous in Miami for riding his bike throughout the city along with all his top staff people. He wasn't sitting in his office reading reports; he was actually out on the street, learning about the community. People saw him, talked to him, shared their concerns with him. That built up trust, confidence, and faith in our police department.

Implementing COMPSTAT helped. Now police officers were able to map trends before they became widespread and devote resources where they were needed. Policing became proactive. COMPSTAT also provided a tool for accountability. Officers had to explain in front of their peers why certain crimes were occurring in their area and what they were doing about it. Information was easier to share. If one part of the city had a strategy to reduce a certain crime, that strategy could now be implemented elsewhere.

We were also able to hire new cops to put on the street. These officers were added as part of our effort to place more cops on the beat who had earlier been assigned to limited or light duty. We increased the size of the civilian workforce to get able-bodied cops out on the street where they belonged. This meant we put many more eyes on the street, including community-based volunteers. People who were previously afraid to talk with police were now helping patrol their own streets through Citizens on Patrol groups. An engaged and cooperative citizenry is a great crime fighting tool.

Additionally, in a city with such a large immigrant population, I am proud that the policy of our police department was to engage the immigrant community in law enforcement, not make them victims of it. Not many cities in America could claim to have first generation immigrants serving as Mayor and Police Chief. Both Chief Timoney and I arrived in the United States in 1961, both from island countries. Together, we achieved secure communities by having immigrants partner with us, instead of hiding from us

No matter was overlooked. Timoney developed a particular interest in traffic fatalities. The chief was amazed to learn that in Miami we had more vehicular homicides than regular homicides. Instead of using crosswalks, the city had people walking across the middle of the street, many of them elderly, being struck by cars. But those are still deaths, preventable ones at that.

Timoney started a two-part campaign, Operation Red Light/ Green Light, to curtail the number of pedestrian deaths and made it a priority for the department. The first part involved education, distributing printed materials, producing public service announcements, and speaking to schools and senior citizen centers. The second involved aggressive traffic enforcement. His efforts paid off, and the number of traffic deaths was reduced by over half. That effort showed the level of concern that Timoney has for human life. Most police chiefs are focused on the major violent crimes, such as homicides, rapes, and robberies. Who talks about traffic accidents? Timoney did.

⬚ ⬚ ⬚

I HAD ANOTHER grand idea—turn Miami from the "Cocaine Cowboy" drug capital into a drug-free city. Operation Difference was Timoney's response. This was a comprehensive operation, earning the respect of the community. Nearly all the components of the police department came into a neighborhood—detectives, DUI enforcement, SWAT, traffic, for example—where they would set up a staging area in a visible location, such as a park. They would then go to work in the area. Each time an operation like this took place, the department would make hundreds of arrests. The residents of the neighborhood could see that the police were making a concerted effort to clear it of the bad guys. It was a holistic approach to getting rid of drug violence, reducing drug use in the city, especially among young people, by 50 percent.

John Timoney also brought his particular qualifications, expertise, and reach in the area of homeland security. There wasn't a single day during my eight years in office that I didn't think of homeland defense. I was part of the class of mayors elected right after 9/11, a day that not only changed history, but rewrote a mayor's traditional job description, making us all the first line of defense against terrorism. I particularly remember being at home one beautiful Sunday afternoon with my family when I received a call from Chief Timoney. A plane headed from London to Miami could theoretically be a terrorist hit, but "we're not sure." This is highly sensitive information and incredibly concerning. Having someone like John Timoney was an added benefit. National law enforcement trusted Timoney enough to let him know what was going on and shared information with him they might not with others. As an expert, he was called on to serve on various national and international anti-terrorism groups. I had someone at my side with ties into that network, who understood what was going on, and could help deal with a crisis situation either before or, God forbid, after an attack. It was reassuring, and felt damned good.

☐ ☐ ☐

YOU CAN ONLY hire so many police officers to cover every corner of a city. Crime fighting and prevention, through improvements to neighborhood quality of life, must therefore extend to every employee of the city. We began by establishing a Quality of Life taskforce. In this multidepartment effort officials from code enforcement, solid waste, fire department, building department, city attorneys, and even the finance department through regulation of occupational licenses partnered with police, the state attorney, and Alcohol, Tobacco, and Firearms (ATF) to help eradicate neighborhood nuisances such as small cafeterias that served food during the day, and at night became places where illegal gambling, drugs, and prostitution were common.

Typically, a guy would get out of work, cash his check, and head down to one of these cafeterias where he would spend his money drinking beer, hanging out with a prostitute, and gambling. Now, he has no money in his pocket and has to go home to his wife. He may hold someone up on the way home to replenish the money he lost, or he may go home and get into a fight with his wife. Now we have a domestic dispute on our hands, requiring police involvement.

During our raids of these cafeterias, several of which I joined, we found not just drugs and weapons, but also rooms in the rear with mattresses and undergarments. Sadly, we also found that many of the female employees were minors. Because of the problems they created, shutting down these illegal cafeterias made sense and became a priority. We were attacking crime at the root. Our raid of the cafeterias also allowed us to confiscate over 300 illegal gaming machines, some of which were later used as evidence by the United States attorney's office to indict and arrest the godfather of the Cuban Mafia after a decade-long investigation. For those who did not fully understand how these illegal activities affected their daily lives, a regular patron of these cafeterias was a man named Reynaldo Elias Rapalo, who turned out to be a serial rapist in Miami's Shenandoah neighborhood.

Getting rid of these cafeterias, bars, and motels also helped reduce the number of prostitutes in the city. We also developed an innovative mapping program. One of the most frustrating aspects of controlling prostitution was that after their arrest prostitutes would be released back to the same street corner where they were picked up. This would usually happen in less time than it took for a police officer to finish the paperwork on the arrest. The mapping program helped correct this problem. Now a judge releases prostitutes on their own recognizance with the condition they are on probation and may not go back to the neighborhood where they were arrested. If they do, they will be arrested not for prostitution, but for violating probation.

The Upper East Side part of Biscayne Boulevard was well known for prostitution. The Boulevard was lined with motels from the 1950s that had decayed over time. As a child, I remember that we would get in the car and take a family field trip to this same area, driving up and down Biscayne Boulevard to look at the motels and their flashy lights. This was a form of free entertainment for a poor family. As the motels became rundown, tourists were replaced with prostitutes and drugs. The mapping program rid the area of prostitutes.

Now, an influx of businesspeople have bought the old motels and are rehabilitating them, along with some of Miami's trendiest restaurants and shops. There is even a Starbucks. I just marvel at driving along Biscayne Boulevard today. When the turnaround began, I would ask my friends to drive to the boulevard for dinner and sit outside at a cafe. "Biscayne Boulevard? Are you kidding me? We're not going down there. What about the prostitutes and drug dealers?"

"Come with me," I'd say. They would join me, and they too would marvel at the transformation. Can you believe this? Where are they, the prostitutes and drug dealers? I don't know, I'd say, but they're not on Biscayne Boulevard.

◻ ◻ ◻

I AM A NEAT FREAK. Whether it's an office or a house or a neighborhood, order and cleanliness says a lot about who you are. So here came another grand idea: I set a goal for Miami to become the cleanest large city in America—a feat no one believed could happen at the time. But we did it. In 2008, *Forbes* Magazine ranked Miami as the cleanest large city in the country. This was a dramatic turnaround from where we used to be. You would drive down city streets and see garbage bags and paper littering them; you would see furniture dumped on the side of the road or in front of a home. This just drove me nuts.

If people drive down a street and see litter, they have no concern with throwing additional garbage out of their car. If everyone else is doing it, you do it too. What difference is one additional hamburger bag going to make to a street already dirty. Yet, when city workers go into a neighborhood and repair a median on a neighborhood street—clean it up and replace the litter with some nice landscaping, trees, plants, flowers—suddenly you don't see a piece of paper on it. People now say, "I'm not going to throw trash here; this is a nice area." This same principle extends to the entire neighborhood and city.

We were the first city in South Florida to invest in automated waste pickup. We gave every household in Miami a new free, green garbage container that can be emptied with a hydraulic arm. This brought uniformity. When I walked during my campaign for mayor and looked down a street, I would see a multitude of different containers or no containers at all: paper bags, plastic bags, different sizes, colors, and shapes. Making matters worse, animals, including rats, would pay overnight visits for dinner. It was, in a word, trashy.

Now, when I look down the street, I see green containers lined up, and nothing else. This helps dramatically in eradicating this image of filth. The new trash trucks had other benefits. The old system relied on back-loader garbage trucks. This kind of truck opens up in the back and the sanitation worker throws the garbage in. Operating the truck requires three people: a driver and two workers on the back who jump on and off to gather the garbage from either side of the street as the truck slowly moves forward. This is labor intensive with three people required to do the job. The city also has to deal with a significant number of worker compensation complaints—someone's back is going out or there are other physical ailments because the workers are picking up large containers of garbage all day long. You also have garbage that doesn't always make it into the truck and ends up spread out throughout the street.

The hydraulic arm truck has only one employee, the driver. The truck pulls up to a house (residents are required to place their containers curbside) and the hydraulic arm picks up the container and empties its contents into the truck. The driver then directs the arm to put the container back down and the truck moves on to the next house. Now you have improved efficiency—one worker is doing the work of three, thus reducing health insurance costs and worker compensation claims. And the streets are cleaner.

What about the two workers previously on the garbage truck? We didn't fire them but reassigned some to conduct daily sweeps of our major thoroughfares, and others to several different parts of the city as part of litter busting teams—rapid response units that would be on call between trash pick-up days. Best of all, city residents and businesses could see the litter busters with their brooms and trash receptacles at work. They understood that the city now cared about cleanliness.

Litter busters also formed part of our graffiti buster teams. As soon as graffiti appeared, they would clean it up—same with illegal dumping. Anyone who saw a sofa or a bookcase dumped on the side of the road could call us, and the litter busters would go out and pick it up as soon as possible. Wherever there was litter, our rapid response teams were there.

Why was all that important? People realized that somebody cared. Those spraying graffiti found that they were fighting a losing battle with us: their messages would be gone almost as soon as they were painted. Although these efforts couldn't entirely eradicate graffiti, our team kept the artists on the move.

There's a certain irony in what happened with our attempt to curtail illegal dumping. Besides litter busters, we also had in place a top-shelf program whereby we picked up large bulky items every week. The surrounding jurisdiction, Miami-Dade County, picks up large items only twice a year at no charge. Any additional pick-ups require a fee from the residents. We started hearing stories about "my cousin coming into the city to put his refrigerator in front of my house on Monday night because he knows Tuesday morning it will get picked up by the city for free." We became a victim of our own success.

▢ ▢ ▢

A CLEAN CITY needs to be a priority. Cities like Seattle and Portland have a long history of being clean and green, ranking at the top in those areas. Then, to everyone's surprise, Miami beat out these traditionally clean cities. I made it a priority, used the mayoral bully pulpit, and our city employees and the people of Miami made it happen. Making cleanliness a priority also made me some enemies.

We started aggressively ticketing people who dumped illegally or put trash out on the curb before the designated pick up time. Trash was not supposed to be put out until after 6:00 P.M. the night before pickup. Some people apparently believed that it was their right to put trash out whenever they pleased, even a week in advance if they were so inclined. So we ticketed the violators. Every time someone received a ticket for violating the trash code they would let me know. But once they received a ticket, they didn't do it again. You have to be committed and willing to take some punches. Maybe one person on the block will be upset, but the rest of the block will be happy. You can't make everyone happy. But if you're committed to something, you can't make exceptions.

Abandoned cars were another form of blight on the city when I first took office. They were all over—thousands—in every neighborhood, including nice neighborhoods. Some were on cinderblocks with their tires missing. Or there might be two or three cars in someone's yard. Again, through a multidepartmental task force, we were able to fix this problem. It bears repeating that my friend former Chicago mayor Richard Daley had advised me that the biggest issue he faced during his first campaign was abandoned cars. He solved the issue in Chicago, and in Miami we no longer have a problem with abandoned cars.

We also turned our attention to illegal housing units. Code enforcement was essential in these efforts and our code enforcement officers worked very closely with the police and building department. My first experience with these units had come during my door-to-door canvassing while running for mayor. I used voter lists to guide me and sometimes I would walk up to a house excited at the prospect of meeting eight voters in one house. That's far better than having to visit eight houses to meet eight individual voters. Then I looked at the surnames. They were all different. What is this? The addresses would be 1001A, 1001B, 1001C, 1001D, etc. The house looked like a maze. The owners of the single-family house had converted it into a multifamily apartment building. Not only was this illegal, it was unsafe and unsanitary. Imagine one garbage can for eight residents. There would be eight cars parked in front of the house taking up spaces that other residents of the neighborhood could not use. It was an absolute disaster for a neighborhood.

We worked to identify and get rid of as many of these illegally converted houses as we could. Again, this was unpopular for some because of the fines levied and the impact it had on the owners' cash flow. But the positive impact on the neighborhood far outweighed any of these concerns.

Finally, there were roosters.

As part of Miami's immigrant population, several of our neighborhoods were home to hundreds of roosters and chickens. These feathered farm animals would walk down the street, fly around, and most annoying of all, serve as 5:00 A.M. alarm clocks. Keeping farm animals within city limits is illegal, but no one wanted to devote the time or resources to enforce these laws. No one cared. We did.

Led by our fire department, the "Chicken Buster" team patrolled our streets, looking for wayward roosters and chickens, using large nets to capture these animals. The team became so popular, that one evening, while watching ESPN's Sports Center, a member of the Chicken Busters was included as part of the "top ten" plays of the week, capturing a rooster mid-flight with a swoop of his net. We ended up capturing over 1,000 roosters and chickens every year, selling them to a local farm, and using the proceeds to purchase Christmas gifts for economically disadvantaged children.

Chapter 11 Investing in Our Future

CITY INVESTMENT STARTS with its neighbor-
hoods. When people read the story of Miami's emergence, they see the
new skyline as a symbol of growth. It is the sexy visual that accompanies
the television or magazine story. But the real story of the reemergence
of a city takes place in its neighborhoods. Creating the attraction that
repopulates a place means that investments must be made to improve
the condition of these places. Fixing streets, improving parks, cleaning
waterways, making common sense transportation choices all combine
to bring people back. If you fix it, they will come.

▢ ▢ ▢

MIAMI NEVER HAD a strategic, long-term capital improvement plan. Sure, repairs were sometimes made, but these were pay-as-
you-go, and usually took place as emergency measures or in the neighborhoods where the district commissioner yelled the loudest. This lack
of planning created chaos, and also negatively affected the city's finances
and bond rating.

As in any business, if you don't see a line item for capital expenses, you don't see the full financial picture: the hidden cost of deferred maintenance. There is a difference between maintaining and repairing. If you perform routine maintenance on your car, for instance, it will tend to last longer. But, if you fail to get an oil change or to perform standard upkeep, the ultimate cost of repairing a breakdown will be much higher. Similarly, we needed a maintenance plan to prioritize where our capital money would go. But first, we needed an actual capital improvements department. That's right, the City of Miami never had one. So, we took existing city employees and staffed our brand new department.

One of the first things we did was conduct an infrastructure study to determine the condition of all city assets. When the results of that assessment came in, they were not pretty. Just in the area of roads, curbs, and gutters, we determined that of the nearly 700 miles of city roads, more than half were rated in poor or critical condition. The estimated cost of these needed improvements was $440 million. Had we continued the practice of allocating only $4 million annually for street improvements, it would have taken 110 years just to redo those streets. That, of course, was an unacceptable time frame.

With a plan in place, we then needed to find the funding. During my 2001 campaign for mayor, I threw my support behind a $255 million bond issue also on the ballot that November. While the bond issue passed, the city did not have any real plans on how to spend the money. Most of the line items were back-of-the-napkin calculations. City officials, in their planning sessions, would say "Ok, park X. Let's give that park a million dollars." But there was no real sense of what that million would buy. Perhaps the needs of that park required much more than a million dollars. A million dollars would be just basically throwing money away, a Band-Aid approach. On the other hand, perhaps the park really didn't need a million dollars for improvements. These weren't real estimates, so we stopped that practice.

The City Capital Improvement Plan became a multi-year effort that included over 700 separate capital projects with a total estimated value of over $765 million. It had a wide ranging impact that reconstruct-ed, resurfaced, and repaired every deficient roadway, sidewalk, and curb in a twelve-year cycle. It encompassed gutters, storm sewers, flood miti-gation, and public and city facilities. It even included, for the first time, traffic calming devices such as traffic circles and raised intersections so that people would no longer speed through city residential streets on their way to and from the suburbs. Traffic circles, or roundabouts, are now found throughout the city and are very popular with residents. It even included a long-term plan to refurbish medians throughout every neighborhood. We tapped other sources that we should have been us-ing for capital as well as receiving a significant amount of money from county, federal, and state sources to leverage our own dollars. Over the course of eight years, we ended up with over $3 billion of capital projects and redid the entire city. After eight years, not a single neighborhood was left untouched by this investment.

And remember all those houses I visited where people would not keep furniture in the front part of their house because of flooding? We helped them too. The Plan devoted over $150 million to flood mitiga-tion with new water pumping stations, drainage, and other measures, alleviating the water hazards that plagued the western neighborhoods. I was able to keep my promise that I would fix the flooding in their streets.

Finally, it was important to me that we rehabilitate every single one of our parks. I took much criticism from a handful of activists about the lack of park space, a reality I inherited from my predecessors and one I very much wanted to change. To that end, after extensive public input, we adopted a Parks and Public Spaces Master Plan. The plan sets forth a very detailed blueprint for the future of Miami's parks system, including the pursuit of the medium-term goal of a park within one-half mile of every resident and the long-term goal of a park within one-quarter mile of every resident.

But before I could even think about new parks, we had to fix the ones we already had. The Plan took $300 million and put it into our parks, in all our neighborhoods. I have stated many times that I grew up playing in parks, and now children from all neighborhoods could enjoy this same luxury. With the leadership of commissioner Joe Sánchez, this included the remodeling of José Martí Park in Little Havana, adding a new state of the art community center and basketball gymnasium. The creation of the Little Haiti cultural park and soccer fields was the dream of late commissioner Arthur Teele. This beautiful complex became the first park built in the Little Haiti neighborhood of Miami, thanks, in large part, to the execution of this dream by commissioner Michelle Spence Jones.

We even modernized facilities, replacing the abandoned and obsolete ping pong tables from the 1970s with new facilities, including Internet access at our major parks. As part of our local cable service contract, we were able to wire all our parks at no cost to the city. The parks were now centers for sports, arts and culture, and digital learning. No matter what their interests, people could find them in our parks. Our efforts at expanding access to parks went as far as building and retrofitting several playgrounds that would accommodate physically disabled children. Miami is the only city in Florida with several such "Boundless Playgrounds," built in a partnership between the city and private sector partners that included the Boundless Playground Foundation and CVS. We were also one of the first cities in the state to receive state funding for this initiative, and we opened three playgrounds, starting with Jorge Mas Canosa Park in Little Havana and Unity Park in Allapattah, both in 2007. Now it is truly possible for all children in Miami to play together in our parks.

Our unprecedented investments led to a dramatic transformation of our parks. In a city that had abandoned its parks, including using some as dump sites for city waste, we doubled the operating budget for our parks. And that leads me to Grapeland Park.

▢ ▢ ▢

GRAPELAND PARK is in a middle-class neighborhood near our airport, represented by commissioner Angel González. When I was elected, the park looked much like it did when I played baseball there as a kid. Time had just passed it by.

The $255 million bond issue for infrastructure repairs had $1.5 million assigned to Grapeland Park. A million and a half dollars would not have gotten you very far, and the amount was calculated without much thought. The old community building looked much the same as when I was a child. It still had two ping pong tables, a couple of bathrooms, and no air conditioning. The facility was in shambles. A million and a half dollars would have probably allowed for construction of new bathrooms and made the building ADA compliant; we might have even been able to put in an air conditioning system. That was about it.

Planning for infrastructure and our ability to leverage funds allowed us to increase that original $1.5 million figure to $40 million. Through a combination of many sources, we were able to create what is today one of Miami's signature parks. In fact, it has become a regional park serving all South Florida. Grapeland now boasts a beautiful water park that takes up about a third of its land. The park has several new baseball fields and tennis courts. It also has the only city-owned golf course in Miami. Before we started our renovations, the golf course did not have a clubhouse; trailers were used instead. It was amazing to me that people would still play golf there. You literally walked in, signed up, played, and then had to leave. If you wanted a coke or beer after finishing a round, it would come out of a cooler. The course was working in spite of these accommodations.

We built a beautiful clubhouse with dining facilities, a bar, bathrooms, lockers, and a pro shop—the kind of facilities you would expect at most golf courses. Next to the clubhouse, a new training facility will have state of the art video equipment and will focus primarily on programs to help low income children learn how to play golf. It will have classrooms and outdoor areas where you can practice your swing, have it taped, and then go into a classroom and study the video.

Our work in Grapeland Park was made more difficult when we found that prior administrations had long ago used the area to dump ash from the city incinerator. The tons of ash we found there had to be removed and the site remediated. It cost between $7 and $9 million to carry out this work before we could even begin to build the water park. Those monies were not in the original budget, but we had to clean the area.

About fifteen blocks from Grapeland is Fern Isle Park, which had the same environmental problems. When I was running for mayor, I actually went to the park, which is alongside a little sliver of a tributary to the Miami River. The park had one baseball field, and beyond the outfield it was undeveloped. The city was using this whole area to dump fill, oil, and other waste. It was yet another trash dump. When I came back to film the dump, I was shocked! A public works truck was parked there, with a city worker sleeping inside it. The video made a great campaign commercial. We also cleaned up Fern Isle Park and built two baseball fields, basketball courts, and picnic areas in the previously contaminated areas.

⬜ ⬜ ⬜

INVESTING IN MIAMI'S water infrastructure is another example of how we leveraged monies and created public-private partnerships that benefited the city, its residents, and the business community. Water infrastructure is a critical government investment. Unfortunately, our federal government, which operates without a national capital plan, places little, if any, emphasis on investments in our water infrastructure. We seem to live under the misguided notion that water will always be there; simply turn on your faucet and clean, potable, and affordable water will always be available.

In Miami, we developed a five-year plan to improve our water quality. The city's water quality was relatively good, but we were seeing runoff from the city, as well as trash and debris going into our drains. This material went into the tributaries flowing into the Miami River and then into Biscayne Bay. Because we challenged city workers to develop innovative solutions to solve these and other problems, I am proud of the fact that it was a public works employee, Francis Mitchell, who developed a filter for our storm drains that could remove trash and debris before it seeped into and contaminated our water system. It was something he designed himself, on his own initiative, that helped protect the water city residents used.

The larger question became how to pay to upgrade our water infrastructure. I found a solution after having a conversation with someone I met through the U.S. Conference of Mayors. Paul Polizzotto had a pilot program in California similar to the Adopt a Highway program, but adopted a waterway not a highway. I wanted to bring the program to Miami, and we became the first city outside California to implement Adopt a Waterway. The Adopt a Waterway program generated a substantial amount of money for us. Business sponsors participating in the program purchased space on custom-designed signs in high traffic areas along city streets. The city received approximately 50 percent of the advertising revenues so generated. We used these funds to pay for storm water pollution prevention projects, including installation of our custom-designed drain filters. Best of all, because we found a way to partner with a private organization, this effort did not cost the City of Miami a penny.

The infrastructure improvement projects that restored the foundations of Miami also included transportation as a key component. Transportation planning was primarily done at a regional level with county and state officials making most of the decisions. Because of this, the city of Miami was in a passive mode when it came to transportation. People were making transportation decisions that affected our city and we had very little to say in that process. I thought, as with other areas in which the city had traditionally not been involved, it was important that we become more proactive.

We started a city transportation office (again, we had never had one) and developed a downtown transportation master plan. The plan included proposals as simple as converting one-way into two-way streets to create a better pedestrian experience that would also help retailers and traffic. Studies show that one-way streets are less friendly to retailers because traffic zips down a street with the drivers paying little attention to the street experience. On two-way streets, the traffic is calmer and the driver is more aware of his or her surroundings, including the retailers that line the street. We ran into some opposition to the conversion, especially at the beginning. There are always hiccups, with people not necessarily happy to make the transition. Once it's up and working and running, people see the benefit and value of it, but not at the beginning. Part of the discontent was the mechanics of making it happen. As much as you prepare, there will always be some wrinkles. But now the system is working fine, and the complaints have disappeared.

In addition to our traffic circle program, the transportation office, working with our capital improvements and public works departments, also worked on small projects to enhance the street experience and provide better transit options. Many of these short-term projects have been implemented, including bus shelters, street furniture, and a bus and trolley system funded through a variety of sources, including the federal stimulus bill. The bus shelter program required coordination with the Miami-Dade County Transit Agency and was another important promise I had made during my campaign. Many of our elderly residents and other transit users had complained about the dilapidated condition of our bus stops and benches. They begged for more comfortable, aesthetically pleasing, and, most important, covered shelters to protect from the rain and heat. We delivered.

The transportation office also worked on significant longer-term transportation plans, including a light-rail street car system. Obviously, these projects are much more challenging because they require significant planning and funding. Still, I'm optimistic that they will be completed. Market conditions will dictate that such projects move forward.

Another long-term project, one of my pet projects when I began my first term as mayor, involved removing or burying an elevated, interstate highway (I-395). As with many other cities, the interstate highway system, concerned only with moving cars and people from point A to point B, left behind many significant neighborhood problems. In our case, I-395's sole purpose was to link people on the mainland with people in Miami Beach. In the process of building it, I-395 sliced through an entire neighborhood in Miami called Overtown. That highway, coupled with the building of I-95, essentially sliced Overtown into four sections, destroying a once thriving Miami neighborhood. Physical barriers like these can eat away and decay any neighborhood. My goal was to depress I-395—either completely tunnel it through an open cut or bring it down to grade. The highway had been poorly designed and had become obsolete from a traffic engineering perspective, and, as a result, it was also unsafe.

The Florida Department of Transportation (FDOT) already had a plan in place to "fix" the highway. Their plan to fix it, however, was to realign I-395, which meant primarily expanding its width. It would then eat into more of Overtown. Again, what happens below the highway was not their concern. I was not going to let this happen. Much to my surprise FDOT, and in particular our regional director, José Abreu, were very cooperative. José put plans on hold until such time as he received additional input from the city and its residents. We began developing a plan to depress the highway to grade level or tunneling it. Numerous design professionals, members of the business community, and residents supported the new plan. Ultimately, neither suggestion was accepted by FDOT primarily because of two factors. One was money; it was a very expensive project and the state didn't have the funding for such an undertaking. The other was engineering and logistics. Overtown itself is not very large geographically. As a result, the highway would have to come down and back out at steep angles that did not satisfy FDOT traffic engineers.

I was not successful in convincing FDOT of my preferred alternative. However, thanks to the cooperation and intervention of José Abreu, we did manage to change FDOT's plans. The new plan would involve demolishing I-395 and replacing it with a safer, higher, and more aesthetic bridge—much like the iconic bridge built as part of the Boston Big Dig project. This alternative is much more attractive and structurally less obtrusive because of the way the tension beams work and the number of structural columns required. The elevated bridge option will not completely reopen the neighborhood of Overtown—in the best of all worlds, nothing would be there in the first place—but it is far less intruding than what is there today. In fact, it may be possible to develop the newly "freed up" areas with retail and green spaces. It is also far less expensive than taking the highway underground.

As I noted previously, market forces will dictate the urgency of moving forward with this project sooner rather than later. The highway feeds an area of Miami that is quickly developing. The Performing Arts Center and Museum Park are there. So is the Miami Heat basketball arena. Two multi-billion-dollar projects may be built in the immediate area, the Miami World Center (described in a prior chapter) and a possible casino destination resort. In its current state, the highway will not be able to properly accommodate all these projects. The new highway is a project that must be done for this area to continue to flourish.

▫ ▫ ▫

THERE IS NO doubt that our unprecedented investments served to strengthen our neighborhoods, create jobs, increase property values, and lower taxes. It also became evident that for Miami to continue growing, investments in other large-scale projects in the urban core would be necessary. Our ability to remain competitive with other world cities depends on these investments. We began with a major transportation infrastructure project for the city: the Port of Miami Tunnel.

The idea for a tunnel had been around since the 1980s and its need has become more acute over time. To access the Port of Miami, you have to drive through the heart of our downtown. That wasn't considered much of an issue when the port was built, but it has since become very significant. New business and residential development required a new approach. On any given day, up to 5,000 18-wheeler trucks are moving in and out of the port. It's a very busy port—one of the busiest, especially for international cargo, in the country. First, the delay to truckers forced to navigate through downtown streets has made the cost of moving their cargo more expensive. As important, imagine the impact of that type of traffic on the urban core. It becomes almost impossible to create a nice urban core with wide sidewalks and cafes as part of a pleasant pedestrian street experience. How can you do that with tractor-trailers traveling the street all day? Getting these trucks off the street was an integral part of establishing the downtown Miami urban core as a place where people want to live. A port tunnel would result in trucks traveling directly to I-395. They would then no longer be required to actually enter the Miami street grid, instead sinking into the tunnel, going to the port, and then coming out through the tunnel and back on to I-395. Congestion would be alleviated, safety enhanced, and the urban core could flourish without truck fumes.

I became involved with the port tunnel project because of my interest in light rail. In thinking about building light rail in the city, I had numerous meetings with my transportation group to determine if we could use rail to move freight into and out of the port. That way it would not be necessary to have trucks enter the downtown area (there was an existing rail line into the port that was rarely used). FDOT told me we couldn't do that. The tunnel project was already in the federal funding pipeline and if the scope of the project was changed, it would be bumped back to the end of the line. That is the way our federal transportation funding system works: when you submit a project for funding, it may take five, ten, or fifteen years or longer to reach the top of the funding list. At that point, the project may have become outdated or obsolete, and certainly much more expensive than originally designed. Ironically, changing the project to make it less expensive or more functional, you risk of losing your place in line. That's the system.

FDOT also indicated that it had researched and rejected various other alternatives. Not being an engineer, I do not possess the expertise to challenge their conclusions. Instead, I was simply trying, as a matter of policy, to push everybody to think in a different direction. This is the same approach I had used to start the debate regarding I-395. At the very least, challenging long-standing assumptions requires the decision makers to take a close second look and reaffirm their initial conclusions. This will often lead to a better result as was the case with the decision of a raised bridge to replace I-395.

Readily available funding for the project was also an important consideration. The state was providing the lion's share of the required funding. However, the failure of local approvals and participation by a certain time meant that the money could be redirected to other projects in the state. Our county government was also providing a significant amount of funding and had approved their participation. The project was budgeted to cost $1 billion, which included a significant contingency factor. The city's required investment was $50 million—not a very substantial investment considering the total project cost—but would be the major beneficiary of the project. As such, I had to argue for the project before the City Commission and make the case that it was economically necessary to the current and future health of the city. A study had been conducted showing that within Miami, the jobs of 18,000 families depended on the port. In South Florida, the number of jobs is 176,000, and the port's estimated economic contribution is $18 billion. I also argued that Dubai had recently invested $300 million to rebuild a port in Mariel, Cuba. So not only does the Port of Miami have competition from domestic ports in Florida (Jacksonville and Fort Lauderdale up the coast), but it now has competition even from Cuba.

To stay ahead of the game and continue to be viable as a port and save all those jobs, we needed to invest our required portion of the project. The Port of Miami is the second-largest job generator behind the airport. If you don't invest in the port to keep it competitive by staying ahead of our competitors, we will lose it, and if we lose it, we lose all those jobs. From an urban planning perspective, from an aesthetic perspective, from an economic perspective, it all made sense. Best of all, the $50 million would come from dedicated funding sources, our community redevelopment area. Our general revenue tax money would not be used, and Miami residents would have no change to their real estate property bill as a result of this investment.

All these arguments were persuasive, but there was a problem—the timing could not have been worse. The County and FDOT wanted the City Commission to approve our participating share immediately or their funding would be withdrawn. They proposed a very tight deadline and pressured me to bring the item to the Commission by September 2007 (September 30 is our fiscal year end, the month during which our budget must be approved). If the Commission voted to reject the proposal, the money would disappear and the tunnel project would be dead. There would not be a second chance. The money would be redirected to another project elsewhere in the state. I advised both the county and FDOT that if they forced me to call for an immediate vote, I could not guarantee its outcome. In fact, my political instincts told me that forcing a vote in September would result in negative Commission action. We were in the middle of budget discussions during a very tough budget year. Programs were being cut and they wanted me to say we would spend $50 million on a tunnel? Even if our contribution would not be derived from our general fund, the political optics of this decision was not the best.

I needed time. But they didn't want to extend the deadline. I made it very clear that there was no way I would present this issue to the Commission for approval unless I had more time. As if a budget crunch and a deadline nearly impossible to meet were not enough, other issues surfaced, including the overall cost of the project and the fact that Bouygues, the French company selected to build the project, apparently had affiliates doing business with Cuba—a lightning rod in Miami politics.

Finally, after going back and forth with the County and FDOT, we decided not to bring it up with the commissioners until December. Yet even that vote might be in jeopardy, since it became clear at that time that only one commissioner, Marc Sarnoff, could be counted on to support the tunnel project. Commissioner Sarnoff represents the urban core. I was afraid that the arguments on the merits of the project were not enough. I needed something more. And that's when I began to design what later came to be known as the "mega plan."

◻ ◻ ◻

THE CITY AND county had been in discussion for decades over a number of pending large-scale projects. Besides the port tunnel, these included a new ballpark for the Florida Marlins (now Miami Marlins), boundary expansions and time extensions for the Overtown and Omni redevelopment areas, a light-rail streetcar system, city contributions to the Performing Arts Center and construction of Museum Park, and relocation of the Miami Art Museum and the Museum of Science to Museum Park. Years of discussion had failed to bring any of these projects to fruition. In fact, the parochial nature of the politics between city and county had prevented the formation of a true partnership essential for the growth of the Greater Miami area. This divisiveness had to change. Clearly, it was to our mutual benefit that we agree on the need to invest in the county seat, Miami's urban core. Fortunately, county manager

George Burgess, with the full support of county mayor Carlos Alvarez, understood this perfectly well.

I sensed that the tunnel issue had presented us with the opportunity to seize the moment, to formalize a partnership around specific projects. Thus was born the mega plan. The idea would be to lump all these projects together as one project. In doing so, we could get the city and county commissioners to vote for the entire basket of projects, rather than approving an individual project such as the tunnel. The basket could include a project opposed by a particular commissioner, but it also included other projects that were priorities for that same commissioner. Voting to approve the mega plan did not guarantee approval of the individual projects. Each project was still subject to public hearings and the approval of both commissions. A commissioner could vote to approve the mega plan, but also choose to vote against a particular project. However, realizing that the agreement carried an unwritten understanding that approval of each individual project by the City and County Commissions was essential to hold the deal together, I felt confident that there would be sufficient support on both commissions to approve all the projects.

The county had long asked the city to contribute funds for the Performing Arts Center. In turn, the city had two redevelopment agencies in that area: Overtown Park West (primarily either vacant, industrial, or Overtown, a historical African American neighborhood), and the Omni (where the performing arts center is located). A Community Redevelopment Area (CRA) is a government tool for redevelopment in Florida; it operates on a budget generated by the increase in property taxes within the area. Once the CRA is established, a percentage of the increase in real property taxes goes to the CRA. This tax increment is used to fund and finance the redevelopment projects identified in the CRA redevelopment plan.

The life of Overtown Park West CRA was expiring somewhere around 2014, but it was just now finally starting to generate tax increment from rising property values. It so far had generated very little such revenue, certainly not enough to do anything substantial to revitalize the neighborhood. Money was going to small projects, nothing of major impact. On the other hand, the Omni CRA was generating serious dollars and we were projecting significant long-term growth for the area. The city very much wanted an extension of the terms and an expansion of the boundaries for these two CRAs.

Remember that Overtown was cut in four by two highways (I-95 and I-395), but only the southeast corner of the neighborhood was part of the redevelopment area. The other three quadrants were left out, so we couldn't take money from the district and spend it in other parts of Overtown. We were limited to just one quarter of the neighborhood. We wanted the county to agree, because they had the statutory authority to do this. We could initiate it, but the county had to ultimately approve a boundary expansion and the time extension of the CRAs. So I made that part of the mega plan. This project was extremely important for the city because it was not just a grand idea; it was about investing in a neighborhood that had gone ignored.

The mega plan had to be put together in a very short period of time. It was finally approved in December 2007. After years of trying and failing, the city and the county agreed, in a three-month period, to go forward on a number of critical infrastructure projects that would generate 25,000 jobs, tens of billions of dollars in economic impact and substantially enhance the future of our region and our city. It should come as no surprise that I personally took a lot of political flack for the mega plan. I was opposed by many civic activists who again cried that I was thinking too big, pushing too large of an agenda. Suits were filed against the mega plan. Those who initiated the litigation would argue that a referendum was required prior to commitment of funds for the projects included in the mega plan. The courts rejected that argument. It was also important to emphasize that the mega plan was but a letter of intent between the county and the city. Projects still had to be approved by both governments at public hearings.

Just to underscore: these half-dozen projects did not come "out of nowhere" after some back room deal. The baseball stadium had generated a tremendous amount of public discussion and debate. The construction of a Marlins baseball stadium had been in the works well before I got elected. There were at least five instances in which the County and City Commissions had approved a baseball stadium deal, only for it to fall apart for other reasons. And in each instance there had been multiple public hearings. As I noted earlier, the Port of Miami tunnel project had been around since the 1980s. It had been the subject of the innumerable public hearings required by the state for a project like this, and had also been on the ballot as part of a countywide election in 2004 where the voters approved expenditure of $100 million for the tunnel project. Funding for the Miami Art Museum and Museum of Science Museum Park (in excess of $275 million) had been voted on by the people of Miami as part of a citywide election in 2001, and was also part of the 2004 countywide election.

These projects had been vetted by the public either through the electoral process or in multiple public hearings dating back decades. Moreover, each component of the mega plan had to be approved separately by each commission, requiring additional public hearings associated with each project included in the mega plan. For the Marlins Stadium alone, the stadium agreement, development agreement, parking agreement, and all the subcomponents of the deal had to be approved individually by the County and City Commissions after public hearings. The criticism that the mega plan amounted to nothing more than a backroom deal of some sort and prevented public participation was without merit—as the Florida Supreme Court made clear when it ruled in our favor.

All the projects have since moved forward. The Port Tunnel broke ground in spring 2011 and the Miami Marlins opened the 2012 baseball season in their new home. The thirty-acre Museum Park is now home to the Miami Art Museum, which broke ground in 2011, and the

Miami Science Museum, which broke ground in early 2012. The Park, originally built in the 1970s and known as Bicentennial Park, was a poorly designed waterfront park without a view of the water. The museums now occupy only eight acres of the site. The remaining twenty-two acres will be built in accordance with the Museum Park Master Plan designed by Cooper, Robertson, and Partners of New York. Museum Park will be Miami's version of Chicago's Millennium Park. Hopefully, a yet-to-be created Museum Park conservatory will be established to operate Museum Park. Across the street, four brand new high rise buildings advertise the advantage of buying a condo in the area because of the surrounding neighborhood: a symphony hall, an opera and ballet house, art and science museums, and a beautiful park overlooking the bay, all within a short walking distance.

When all these projects are completed, Miami's waterfront will have few rivals in the world. We will have created an entirely new urban core for Miami. That is where you go when you visit a city: the urban core, with its museums, its arts centers. When as mayor you say: I want to rebuild the city, bring residents into the city, and populate a 24/7 downtown Miami, you have to have, besides fundamentals like safety and infrastructure, the amenities for residents to enjoy so that they want to live there.

Over the length of my term, and despite the detractors, the combined public investment into City of Miami infrastructure came close to $10 billion, while reducing the tax rate on city residents by over 20 percent. From the streets, sidewalks, bridges, and parks of our neighborhoods, to tunnels, museums, and stadiums, we essentially rebuilt the city. Today, when you drive through Miami, things don't look broken anymore. And people have noticed, by reversing the decline in population. Miami's population increased by double digits from the time I took office, with the most dramatic impact in the urban core. What was once a dead downtown is now a 24/7 population center. During the decade 2000–2010, almost 100 high-rise residential buildings were built in downtown Miami. The downtown population now exceeds 70,000 residents, almost 60 percent ages twenty to forty-four. Retailers including restaurants have followed, and new residential and retail projects are underway or have been announced. The investments described in this chapter and throughout the book helped rebuild our neighborhoods, the urban core and Miami's skyline. Miami is now mentioned in the same breath and category as other world cities. Invest in your future, and it will pay dividends.

ALL MAYORS FACE significant challenges: combating poverty by increasing economic opportunity, ensuring the safety of their residents, bringing quality education to their children, and creating opportunity for all, especially at times when people are suffering the loss of their jobs, their homes, their businesses. Sometimes city design gets lost in all that. Yet, a mayor's role to make cities sustainable, to make them work, is more important today than ever, as the world is becoming more urban. Mayors must become the architects of their city's future.

For the first time in history, over half the world's population live in cities and metropolitan areas. In the United States, it is 85 percent. Our metro areas drive the world's economies, generating over 90 percent of all jobs, income, and GDP generated by cities. Traditionally, American cities developed as high density, compact, walkable, mixed-use neighborhoods. Think of Manhattan, Georgetown in D.C., and Beacon Hill in Boston. After World War II, this all changed as people abandoned cities for the suburbs. On their way out, they paved our land, destroyed our natural areas, spent billions on superhighways to connect distant neighborhoods, and strained municipal budgets.

Worst of all, we glorified the automobile. People now face longer commutes, traffic congestion, more asphalt, pollution, and increasing human impact on climate change. The average American household spends more on transportation than on food and health care combined, with more than four billion hours annually in traffic instead of with their families. This is why the single most critical response to help keep our country strong is to embrace smart growth—to design cities that make sense.

□ □ □

MIAMI IS KNOWN for lots of great things—our beaches, culture, restaurants, nightlife, and diversity. What we had not been known for is being a leader in the environmental movement. That was left to cities in the Pacific Northwest and the Northeast. I remember that when I first began to talk about green buildings, most people thought, "Manny's gone crazy; he wants us to paint all our buildings green." The fact is Miami's history is filled with examples of an almost criminal neglect for our environment, including dumping waste into our parks, as I described in Chapter 11.

Well, things have changed. And they had to change because we couldn't ignore the fact that, if we were to continue enjoying the natural beauty that surrounds us, we needed to take steps to preserve it. Miami is the only major metropolitan area in the nation surrounded by two national parks—the Everglades to our west, Biscayne Bay to our east. We are also in the middle of Hurricane Alley. The effects of climate change should therefore be very real to us. So we set out to respond through a citywide climate action plan.

We created our first ever Office for Sustainable Initiatives and formed a Green Commission that included members of the community. We facilitated the LEED (Leadership in Energy and Environmental Design) accreditation of many of our city employees, instituted expedited permitting for LEED buildings, and began green procurement and water conservation measures. We started a "green lab" to promote environmental innovation, and greened several of our schools. We even installed solar panels at City Hall.

We built miles of bike lanes and adopted the city's first Bicycle Master Plan. We created Bike Miami, a once-a-month event during which numerous streets throughout the urban core were closed to cars, with only bicycles, tricycles, pedestrians, and skates permitted. There is no doubt that through the plan, activities like Bike Miami, and my bully pulpit, the number of cyclists in the city has increased exponentially during the last few years, a condition I happily witness firsthand to and from work every day. We also began the process of converting our city fleet to green vehicles. I switched my city-issued SUV for a hybrid, cut gas consumption in half, and passed the savings to taxpayers.

In a city where hurricanes depleted our tree canopy, we implemented a Tree Master Plan and a Landscape Ordinance, allowing our canopy to be increased in all neighborhoods of the city in order to achieve our goal to increase it to 30 percent by 2020. I am very proud that for the first time ever, Miami was named a Tree City USA by the Arbor Day Foundation. All these steps, while important, still did not ensure long-term sustainability of Miami, so we had to do more.

We then took the ultimate and most comprehensive step toward sustainability by dramatically increasing the density of our city, because bringing people back to the urban core is the ultimate antidote to suburban sprawl. Every residential condo built in downtown Miami means one less residential suburban development encroaching on the Everglades. The need for urban density and smart growth created Miami 21: sustainability through design.

▢ ▢ ▢

THROUGHOUT ITS HISTORY, Miami grew without a plan to direct or manage growth. During our research, we found an article from the turn of the last century in which city fathers rejected the idea of a master plan as "too expensive." The cost? $1,000. It ended up costing us much more than that in the long run. Had that investment been made, Miami would have grown in a way that makes sense. Instead, we had haphazard growth. It was a planning philosophy of "build now, plan later" or not at all.

I started developing the concept of a master plan for the city during my campaign for mayor. But I had no idea about urban planning or smart growth or any of the principles I would learn about later. All I knew is that when I looked around Miami, intuitively I saw much that didn't make sense. I also knew that if we were to put our other plans in place and tap into the unrealized potential of the city, new development and people would follow. This would require a plan for growth that had to go beyond zoning: not merely swapping one zoning code for another, but a holistic approach with parks, green spaces, transportation, the arts, and historic preservation all working together to create a sense of place. My idea was to create the blueprint for the Miami of the twenty-first century and beyond: Miami 21.

We started the Miami 21 process by working with Ana Gelabert-Sanchez, city planning director, and her staff, led by Luciana González. They were terrific. Now we needed to put a team in place to execute the plan. I very much wanted Elizabeth Plater-Zyberk and Andrés Duany to captain this team. They had outstanding international reputations in developing the principles of the New Urbanism. New Urbanism is a return to planning that creates and promotes walkable, neighborhood-based development as an alternative to sprawl. As an added bonus, they were Miamians. Andrés is Cuban American and Liz is dean at the University of Miami School of Architecture. Although they both live and work in Miami and have projects all over the world, they weren't doing any work in their hometown. Additionally, and this is important, they did not represent individual clients in the city. As a result, I did not have to worry that they would lose or gain clients from whatever recommendations they were making. Residents could feel comfortable they were independent thinkers who had been espousing a particular philosophy for some time. They wouldn't be beholden to the development community or to any politician. From every perspective they were the right people for the job.

The most effective way to implement New Urbanism is to incorporate its principles into zoning and development codes. However, this had never before been tried in a city the size of Miami with an existing built environment. Bringing New Urbanism to Miami was a radical change from the way the city had grown during its first hundred years.

We had an idea and a team in place. Now it was time to fund the project—and it took at least a couple of budget cycles to achieve the funding necessary to hire the planning crew and finally begin to work. We kicked off Miami 21 officially in April 2005 with a large public event in downtown Miami. We invited a variety of people: architects, neighborhood residents, everybody—and everybody showed up, 700 of them, on a Saturday, at 8:00 A.M. I asked Mayor Joe Riley from Charleston, South Carolina, to give the keynote speech because his nationally recognized leadership in urban planning had inspired me to do the same in Miami. Richard Rosan, former president of the Urban Land Institute, was also invited and addressed the group.

We started working on the various components of the plan right away. While Miami 21 grew from my strong belief that a city should plan for its future, by mid-decade it took on a whole new added value and dimension. What had begun as an urban planning exercise had become an integral part of the fight against global climate change.

In 2005 the Kyoto accords went into force, requiring industrialized nations (but not the United States, since it was not a signatory) to reduce their greenhouse gas emissions to help stave off global warming. A year later Al Gore's film *An Inconvenient Truth* helped galvanize the nation's attention about the dangers of not doing anything about global climate change. Because of our federal government's failure to act on this matter, former mayor of Seattle Greg Nickels developed the U.S. Mayors Climate Protection Agreement as a way for mayors to implement the Kyoto accords in their cities. Over 1,000 mayors from the entire political spectrum have signed the agreement.

The Climate Protection Agreement placed a heavy emphasis on urban planning—especially land use. Now, when we connected urban planning to our cities' carbon footprint and greenhouse gas emissions, environmental concerns took on a new meaning. The agreement also singled out land use as the most important factor to consider in implementing a city's climate protection plan.

Miami 21 now took on a whole new significance in my mind. I also realized that if we began to promote its environmental positives, people would see the connection and no longer dismiss or criticize the plan as simply a zoning code overhaul. It became an effort to promote environmental sustainability. At the same time, it would become an economic development tool, bringing jobs closer to our residents through the creation of zoning categories that promote live-work and others that permit low scale, mixed-use developments throughout the city. This demonstrates the way that a mayor takes on new duties as the world changes. Just as 9/11 turned mayors into first responders for homeland security, we also became the first responders to global climate change. Miami 21 provided a significant response to climate change, and I wanted to make sure it was a response open to and driven by citizen participation. It was also important in that it revolutionizes the way planning is approached.

Miami 21 is a planning document as much as a land development regulation code. While most codes are typically prohibitive in nature (they tell what you cannot do), I wanted a code that told you what we wanted you to do. The smart growth principles of Miami 21 allow you to determine where growth will take place, promote the areas where it is meant to occur, and, in the process, protect historic single family neighborhoods.

□ □ □

WE STARTED WITH an idea born of a desire and the need to plan our future, to realize our collective vision for a better city: one where we preserve the valuable elements of our past; where we respect the unique character and enhance the elements of our neighborhoods; where we support future environmental and economic sustainability. We then went out and started to solicit input from the people of Miami.

Close to 500 public meetings were held in one form or another. Such public awareness, participation, and input were crucial in the development of the plan. We began a full-scale public relations and media campaign with printed materials, website and email marketing, promotional products, and an advertising component that further increased public awareness. The team even developed a grassroots campaign aimed at diversifying outreach, making sure all Miami's communities had input into the plan.

Numerous newspaper articles provided extensive coverage of Miami 21 from its launch, highlighting the plan through local, regional, and national exposure. Email messages were very effective in reaching stakeholders with project updates and upcoming meeting information to over 4,000 subscribers. The website also played a key role in the public process by creating a platform where residents could submit questions and comments. Individual responses were posted on the site for the benefit of all. We even started a Miami 21 hotline. This hotline allowed callers to listen to recorded messages about the projects. You could reach operators that gave you information in Spanish or Creole with an offer to send more information via mail for those that did not have access to the web or email. The outreach effort transformed the planning process from a passive one in which citizens have government actions imposed on them, to one in which people became involved in the process and had a direct interest in the outcome.

In the end, Miami 21 was not written by lawyers and special interests so that only lawyers and special interests could understand the zoning laws. It became a plan written by all the people who participated in the public meetings and on our website, with more than a quarter million unique visitors, over 4,000 subscribers, and 7 million hits. It is the most democratic planning document in our city's history.

The people's voice was reflected in three important goals that emerged for Miami 21:

1. Protecting our neighborhoods;
2. Enhancing neighborhood livability; and
3. Achieving environmental and economic sustainability.

Miami 21 will protect neighborhoods through successional zoning that promotes controlled and planned growth. Zoning decisions will no longer focus on a specific piece of land, but must be made in the context of the surrounding neighborhood. Zoning changes will only be considered twice a year, preventing the struggles we witnessed monthly during zoning hearings when, more often than not, those with the money to afford lawyers who know the code won, while our neighborhoods and our people lost.

Miami 21 takes into account the entire neighborhood—with emphasis on the preservation of historic community assets (through transfer of development rights), preservation of neighborhood scale, integration of density transitions for protection of low-density residential neighborhoods, and reduction of floor plates for multifamily residential and commercial high-rise buildings. Its design requirements ensure compatibility with neighborhoods, preventing many of the offensive buildings, McMansions, and Big Box stores that used to go up without any review. These and many other protections will bring neighborhood zoning decisions that we all want and that make sense.

Miami 21 will also enhance the qualities of neighborhoods that make them come alive, giving them a sense of community, a sense of place—as in most planned cities. Paying attention to streetscapes, stoops, driveways, tandem parking, garage width, setbacks—and bringing back the front porch—creates the sort of places that produce a significantly higher quality of life. Miami 21 encourages growth that is desired rather than coerced through zoning variances, showing what we want our streets, neighborhoods, and city to look like, and creating an atmosphere that encourages walking, cycling, and personal interaction. It will get rid of the current practices that blight our streets and make them uninviting to residents and visitors. Parking uses will be lined with residential or commercial spaces that help enhance and support the development of commercial corridors. Buildings will be placed at the street edge, rather than behind a sea of surface parking, thus enhancing our city's sense of place. It also requires active ground floor uses that animate streets, create a sense of safety and minimize conflicts, finally making the public realm pedestrian friendly. These are the factors that improve and enhance the quality of life of a neighborhood. Miami 21 respects people and encourages our ability to live among one another in places that are designed to make interaction easier, making our sense of community stronger.

Finally, and equally important for our future, Miami 21 supports the continued economic and environmental sustainability of our city. Ensuring a sustainable future means we must plan not around cars, but around people. It reflects a growing desire among residents for a lifestyle that includes vibrant mixed-use, live-work, and walkable communities with varied transit choices—a lifestyle not allowed by the previous code and many codes throughout the United States.

In Miami, a city with an enviable year-round climate, no one liked to walk. It's not that it's "too hot" to walk, as the arguments went. Places like New York, Washington, and Chicago all have hot summers, but they also have beautiful, active, and inviting streets to enjoy. Wider sidewalks, active and inviting frontage, shade trees, bicycle lanes, alternative and viable transportation, green and civic spaces, and consideration of how light and air interact with the street below not only invite us out of our cars, but promote the walking experience, creating streets and neighborhoods that respect and are centered around people. Miami 21 also affects physical space through green building techniques that bring energy conservation and promote greater use of open public and civic spaces. In fact, it may be the only code that provides regulations for the public realm, not just private property.

The Public Benefits program also recognizes that Miami's continued economic well-being requires a wide range of housing choices at prices accessible to individuals at all income levels. This element of Miami 21 seeks to encourage the development of communities that reflect Miami's rich racial, ethnic, and economic diversity, strengthening the diversity that makes us who we are as a city.

The Public Benefits Trust Fund was a uniquely innovative approach. It provided incentives while promoting affordable housing, parks, and open space. It provided developers with options to meet their bonus requirements by building on their property or other areas of need or by simply making a contribution to the fund. Additionally, the fee for the bonus is designed to be representative of the land/construction value of each neighborhood and is reviewed by a third party annually in order to allow for changes in the economy. The Public Benefits Program has proven to be an attractive feature for developers and a more effective alternative to inclusionary zoning.

▢ ▢ ▢

CLEARLY, MIAMI 21 not only implements the principles of sustainability through smart growth, but also is a radical departure from the old Euclidean Code (named after a court case that upheld the right of the government of Euclid, Ohio, to impose zoning under its police powers) that had governed development in Miami until Miami 21's adoption. The Euclidean code in Miami was a typical code that many cities still use. It is, however, very restrictive. A residential building must be zoned residential. An office building may be used only for offices and a commercial building only for commercial use. There are no mixed uses, which is an impediment in terms of creating a pedestrian friendly, walkable, mixed-use community. But that kind of community is what we should want. Residents want to be able to walk outside where they work or live and find a grocery store or dry cleaner. This is the way cities functioned in the past. Euclidean zoning changed this by segregating uses. It was designed to keep manufacturing in one part of the city, residential in another, and so forth. Conversely, a form-based code like Miami 21 is designed for the green city of the twenty-first century.

I would venture to say most cities don't have sequential transitions—the transect—to guide development. The transect is the building block of New Urbanism, and, in turn, fundamental to Miami 21. We use the transect to develop zoning areas that naturally progress from the rural to the urban core. In most towns and cities, areas are zoned R1, R2, R3 residential: R1 is a single-family home; R2 is two-family; R3 is a little more dense, and so on. Transects are identified as T1, T2, T3. T1 is a rural, natural area such as the Everglades. T6 is the urban core. We transit from natural areas to intense density. The zoning is sequentially increased.

Under the old residential zoning concept, it was possible to zone parcels next to each other in a scheme that was anything but sequential. One parcel might be zoned R1, with a single-family home, and the parcel next to it might be zoned commercial, which could be a multistory building. This, combined with the bonuses described below, created conflict among residents and developers in Miami. At the same time, the city had put in place, at the behest of developers, a number of archaic principles that didn't get noticed until Miami began to grow. Since no one was building in the city, no one could see the practical application of some of the "ideas" the development community had asked for and the city had implemented with the intention of creating incentives for Miami to grow.

Now Manny Diaz comes around, development starts, and the past's Band-Aid approaches become apparent. I get blamed for much of that because somehow I'm supposed to stop some of this bad and haphazard development. Yet the development was taking place under the laws that existed on the books for close to twenty years. With respect to property rights, the mayor can't tell someone, "You can't build that; I don't like this project." Furthermore, some projects were executed under passive rights; the developers did not have to bring their projects to the planning department for review. They only had to secure a building permit and start immediately.

This history helps explain why, during my time in office, high-rise buildings could be built next to someone's single-story house. This long-standing practice permitted developers to build taller by counting land outside their lot. This proved to be a major source of irritation for residents. The old code, through much lobbying by the development special interests and acquiescence from past city administrations, allowed developers to gross up lots so that they could count the surrounding area for determining how high they could build. What was the result of this concession?

Here is a hypothetical example under the old code. Let us determine how tall a building one can build on a given lot by measuring the size of the lot and multiplying it by a factor known as the floor area ratio. This measurement should provide maximum building capacity. But now with grossing up, the fun begins. Depending on how many streets a lot fronted, a builder could count to the middle of the street to increase the lot's size. Next to a public facility like a park, the builder could count to the middle of the park so the lot grew some more. And if it's next to Biscayne Bay, the builder can claim ninety feet into the water, so the lot grows even more. But, we're not done. As if this were not enough, the city threw in a free 25 percent bonus and one could get another 20 percent by making a contribution to the affordable housing trust fund. With those additions to the base lot, suddenly the lot has now artificially ballooned to double the size. Thus, it was perfectly legal to construct a fifty-story building next to that single-family home.

This is a difficulty that we faced. I went out to promote development in Miami, and for the first time we began to experience the practical effects of the archaic laws and practices of our predecessors. Despite how any one of us felt about this, it was the law. Our hands were tied, so we changed the law. Miami 21 has eliminated grossing up of lots. Now, you count the size of the lot and that's it. Obviously we're working with a built environment and not starting from scratch, which means Miami 21 makes an effort to preserve existing property rights, but the game stops.

Now a developer can only change things sequentially. You cannot come in and get one property rezoned. Any change to the character of a property must be done sequentially, because this is the direction the neighborhood is taking. When you start at a T4 (a three-story building), you can only go up to a T5 (a five-story building). Making that change means changing the entire neighborhood, not just one parcel. Moreover, the developer or builder would have documented during a public hearing that the area needs a building different from what is in the neighborhood and would proceed only after the neighborhood has agreed to the change. The case of sporadic zoning change will not happen again. Now the design of a building, constructed under Miami 21, will be completely different. Buildings will have context and relate to neighborhoods, things will start to make sense.

Miami 21 replaced the incertitude of the old building code, where lawyers, lobbyists, and special interests controlled development. The people of Miami gave their input into what they wanted our city to look like, and Miami 21 provides the certainty to make that vision a reality. It also makes sense to developers because a project that complies with Miami 21 is no longer subject to a lengthy and expensive public process. We have taken the risk and arbitrary nature from the old code and replaced it with certainty of development rights.

◻ ◻ ◻

ONE FINAL AND very important aspect of Miami 21 is its encouragement of "green" building. Two fundamental factors contribute to greenhouse gas emissions: buildings and cars. We have already discussed the importance of getting people out of their cars and walking. Miami 21 also requires that all private and public buildings 50,000 square feet or more in higher density zones be built, at a minimum, LEED silver certified. The code gives bonuses if you go above silver. This is a very significant standard, one that only a few cities in America have. Miami went on to become home to the first pre-certified LEED building in the state. In fact, while in the middle of the last decade we had zero green buildings, we now have over 110 LEED certified buildings in South Florida. Our message was simple: build green, or don't build at all. And while protecting our environment is a necessary and laudable goal, it also has to make financial sense to the building developers. Green is associated with environmental awareness, but it also means money. Green is good for business and good economics.

After I left public office and returned to my law firm, we chose to move to a LEED silver building on Brickell Avenue. As late as 2010, this building was not LEED certified, but now it was. Why is that? The building's anchor tenant, another law firm, moved downtown to a brand new LEED gold building. Just down the street on Brickell, another LEED gold building opened, also landing a major law firm as a tenant. Landlords and tenants are choosing LEED because it makes sense.

When these real estate professionals, developers, architects, engineers, and building managers all pitch LEED to clients or tenants, they don't sell them on reducing greenhouse gas emissions 50 percent by 2050. They talk about reducing long-term operating and occupancy costs. They don't show pictures of melting glaciers in the Arctic. They explain how LEED helps improve the health and productivity of employees; how it increases tenant retention. They discuss faster absorption and higher rents. They don't admonish potential clients for increasing the severity of our weather if they choose to go non-LEED. Instead they show them how LEED increases the marketability, cap rates, and resale value of buildings.

Green has to make business sense. This was my pitch to developers when we first made green building a priority. The upfront costs are only nominally higher, but they are more than offset on the back end. And yes, this is vitally important for the future sustainability of our planet—and for the future of our children and grandchildren.

Rob Hink, former president of the South Florida Chapter of the U.S. Green Building Council, reminded me of a story that illustrates this point. Rob helped me organize a series of forums for real estate professionals designed to convince them of the merits of going green. We brought green professionals from across America to share their experiences with their Miami colleagues. A local developer, Alan Ojeda, who built the gold certified 1450 Brickell, attended one of those forums and later approached Rob to tell him, "Now I get it." Although Alan walked in a skeptic about the science and the economics, now he will never ever again develop a non-green building. He understood the benefits to his bottom line and is also now proud to extol his efforts on behalf of saving our planet.

▫ ▫ ▫

MIAMI 21 IS the most exciting project I worked on. If I had to do it all over again, I would. While many other cities have adopted form-based principles to areas such as a waterfront or a specific neighborhood, we were the first to do so on a citywide basis. John Hickenlooper, former mayor of Denver and now governor of Colorado, came to Miami in 2005 to study several aspects of the city, including Miami 21. Denver then adopted a form-based code very similar to ours. It makes me proud that we were able to lead in this area.

My staff told me on several occasions that I should just walk away from Miami 21, that it was too much heavy lifting, taking up too much of my time and political capital. They even questioned whether I would have enough votes from the City Commission to get it done. I always kept fighting, because this is a very important legacy for Miami. If it was ultimately defeated, it would not be because I quit. So I kept pushing, and in the end Miami 21 was approved at the last Commission meeting of my second term. The vote was 4-1. Miami made a clean break with its past of environmental neglect and lack of planning. Greatness cannot be achieved without proper planning; if you fail to plan, plan to fail. That's why we invested in Miami 21.

In 1906, when David Burnham produced a plan for Chicago, he inspired us with these words: "Make no little plans; they have no magic to stir men's blood and probably themselves will not be realized. Make big plans; aim high in hope and work, remembering that a noble diagram once recorded will never die, but long after we are gone be a living thing."

In Miami, we were not afraid to dream big dreams, to aim high in work and hope. We took a step back for the sake of our future, to control our destiny, and in doing so set a course to guarantee our sustainability— a future that embraces the opportunity to enhance the beautiful and generous public realm, the spaces that create pride, that are equally owned by our residents, irrespective of economic and social circumstance. These are grand ideas. We dreamed big and aimed high, because we owe a lasting legacy to those who will call Miami home long after we are gone.

Chapter 13 Fostering Arts and Culture

MIAMI NEEDED A STRONG and vibrant cultural arts life similar to what is found in other major world cities. That void made it difficult to attract people. It also struck me very personally that we needed these opportunities because I had developed a deep appreciation for the arts at an early age, when I was strongly influenced by the humanities curriculum of the schools I attended. I wanted children in Miami to have the same opportunities, the same exposure to art and culture that children in other cities do.

I began with this idea: a great city like Miami deserves great places of art. Not only do the arts generate thousands of jobs and billions of dollars in tourism, but art is one of the few areas of civic life with low barriers to entry. It builds ties between neighbors and communities that become particularly important in a city with such a diverse population.

Elected officials who promote investing in the arts and culture typically face political criticism. Most of this stems from the mistaken belief held by some that arts are for the well-to-do, for the "wine and cheese crowd" as they are called. I was criticized as well. In Miami, it was not politically popular to push for the arts. Some local politicians questioned investing in the arts, presenting a false choice. "We should spend money on fixing potholes, not on museums," they would say. We did both. To say that art is reserved for the rich, or to suggest that the poor do not care about art and culture simply because of their economic status, is more than empty rhetoric. It is dehumanizing, bigoted, and just plain wrong. Every citizen of Miami, especially our poorer children, deserves the best we can give them—including access to the arts. As with many of our grand ideas, they begin in our neighborhoods.

◻ ◻ ◻

MY FIRST ARTS initiative was the Hearts of Our Parks, an after school and summer arts program. The program's creator was a member of my staff, Michelle Spence Jones, now a City of Miami commissioner. The parks I grew up in were really about playing sports. If you wanted to paint or sing or dance, your parents could pay money to get you lessons or enroll you in private music camp. It just wasn't something you could do in a park. We wanted to change this. Parks became centers of culture. We started by turning the facilities into art and dance studios, offering dance, singing, painting, crafts, and lessons in other art forms. These lessons then started blossoming into ensembles and other performance opportunities. Singing lessons led to the formation of the Miami Children's Choir (which released its own CD with the help of the University of Miami School of Music). We had a band camp. We even worked with the Florida Film Institute to create a film program to engage students in the creative visual arts.

At the end of every summer, the children who had participated in the arts program would get the opportunity to showcase all they had learned by participating in a recital. They would stage plays, show movies they made, play in their bands, or sing with their choirs. It was great to see kids of all ages and economic backgrounds—from the very young to high school students—showcasing their newly learned talents. Their families would be there too, telling us through teary eyes how grateful they were for this opportunity. When school funding was being cut, especially for arts and after-school activities, we stepped in and gave these children the opportunity to access the arts. And it was free to the parents. Parks then became places to show free movies, free concerts, even Shakespeare plays. That was my initial effort to get arts into the neighborhoods, to make sure it wasn't a wine and cheese thing. Art is for everybody.

▢ ▢ ▢

TO PROVIDE a means of expression for Miami's diverse communities, we supported and expanded the number of neighborhood art fairs and community theaters. This was especially important in keeping the cultural identity of neighborhoods, for art is an expression of who we are, especially for immigrant communities. For example, Little Haiti saw the opening of the Little Haiti Cultural Center, which is a gem. Its black box theater served as the site for many of the recitals that took place for members of the Heart of our Parks programs during the summer. Little Havana became home to Viernes Culturales—Cultural Fridays—a monthly street party and art walk to showcase Cuban and Latin American art and galleries. Little Havana also saw the restoration of two neighborhood theaters, the Tower and Manuel Artime, both of which had fallen into disrepair and had closed, but which now serve as venues for the Miami Film Festival (Tower) and for live musical and theater performances (Manuel Artime).

Restoration of local community theaters also meant that the historic Lyric Theater in Overtown received a facelift. This theater was built by one of Miami's first black millionaires in the 1910s and anchored a section of town called "Little Broadway," where black performers (Count Basie and Ella Fitzgerald among them) who were not allowed to stay in hotels on Miami Beach (in spite of being allowed to perform there) found a home and stage. The Lyric Theater was a great source of pride to the African American community and is once again open as a home to the arts.

A similar fate had befallen the Olympia Theater in the heart of downtown Miami. Originally built as a grand scale movie palace in the 1920s, the theater was saved from demolition by Miami philanthropist Maurice Gusman in the 1970s and renamed in his honor. Gusman Theater, as it is now known, is listed on the National Register of Historic Places and after its renovation currently hosts a wide range of musical performances from classical to pop.

The Freedom Tower has also been restored thanks to the efforts of Pedro and David Martin and to those of the current owner of the facility, Miami Dade College. As described in Chapter 1, this building is a Miami landmark. The Martins, local developers, had acquired a parcel of land that included the Freedom Tower. Through their generosity (and some insistence from the mayor), the building was donated to the College, which converted it into an arts and cultural mecca, hosting events such as a Salvador Dalí exhibit. In order to promote the arts in Miami, I used the Freedom Tower as the backdrop for an important conversation with a very special guest, best-selling author and journalist Tom Wolfe. Tom and Chief Timoney were friends from their days together in New York. Taking advantage of this relationship, I invited Tom to speak to the citizens of Miami about the important role of the arts in developing and revitalizing cities and neighborhoods.

Everyone has a theory on what makes cities succeed. During one of our conversations, Chief Timoney proudly proclaimed his theory. Of course, it is the police that allow citizens and business to flourish in a city. "Nonsense," retorted Wolfe. "It's the artists! These are the urban pioneers that go into edgy neighborhoods and establish the outpost."

The expansion of art into our city neighborhoods led to the creation of arts and culture districts throughout the city. To Wolfe's point, artists are usually at the forefront of neighborhood revitalization, and in Miami it is no different. However, we had to make sure the conditions were ready for investment and attractive to artists and other creative people. Besides cleaning up the streets and making the neighborhood safe (Timoney's point), we provided economic incentives that made it easier to open businesses such as restaurants in these districts.

Then, just as I convinced developers to invest in Miami, I did the same with prominent art collectors. Take Wynwood, for instance. This area that borders both Midtown Miami and the Design District now has over one hundred art galleries, and is home to some of the most important art collections in the world. When I was first elected mayor, Wynwood was yet another neighborhood the city had neglected in the past. It was also too unsafe for a leisurely walk. Needless to say, it was also not a place for art galleries.

The Rubbell Family Collection (and its founders Don and Mera Rubbell) was already housed in a 45,000 square foot repurposed Drug Enforcement Agency confiscated goods facility. Frustrated by past city neglect, they were threatening to leave Wynwood. Thanks to Commissioner Winton's leadership, we convinced one of the largest privately owned contemporary art collections in the world to stay in the neighborhood.

Gary Nader now has an incredible space in Wynwood. When I first met him, he was in Coral Gables, a suburb of Miami. I told him Wynwood would become the new arts place—it's Chelsea, SoHo, Tribeca rolled into one. You need to go into Wynwood. And he did! Gary now has one of the largest collections of Colombian artist Fernando Botero's work in the world. And he has built a massive gallery of nearly 100,000 square feet to house the work he exhibits.

Ella Cisneros opened a gallery close to the University of Miami in the Coral Gables area. At the opening and on our first meeting, I told her the same thing I told Gary, you need to be in Wynwood. "Where's Wynwood?" she asked. She now has a beautiful place in the Park West Wynwood area. And so, little by little, people have come into the area. What were once the white walls of empty industrial warehouses and factories now feature the works of some of America's best graffiti artists.

Tony and Joey Goldman are a pair of Wynwood pioneers. The Goldmans helped in the revitalization of SoHo and South Beach. They saw the potential in Wynwood and immediately jumped on board, buying several parcels of land in the area, and even set up one of the best pizza places in the city. During a visit to Miami for a concert, U2's lead singer Bono put his imprimatur on Wynwood, stopping by the Goldmans' restaurant for a bite to eat.

Wynwood feeds off Midtown Miami and the Design District, all adjoining neighborhoods, to create an art/design/living area. A resident of Midtown can walk over to Wynwood and see the latest in art, or go shopping in the Design District, all creating the walkable neighborhood energy that was missing from Miami, and certainly from that area. The revitalization of the Design District was spearheaded by another pioneer, Craig Robins, who had also played an integral role in the repositioning of Miami's South Beach district. Craig and his team have helped revitalize this once abandoned and unsafe neighborhood into one of the most important global centers for cutting edge art, design, antiques, fashion, night life, and restaurants.

Through our efforts to create these districts, other neighborhoods in Miami—such as Little Havana, Little Haiti, Coconut Grove, Downtown, and Overtown—continue to emerge as arts destinations. Our efforts to promote arts and entertainment throughout the city mean that on any given weekend in any of Miami's neighborhoods, there is an art or cultural event taking place.

▢ ▢ ▢

WHILE WORKING TO make art an integral part of every neighborhood, we were able to capitalize on a major moment in the history of arts in South Florida: the arrival of Art Basel in Miami. Held in Basel, Switzerland, Art Basel is the largest art fair in the world. The sponsors wanted to expand their art fair to the Western Hemisphere, so in December 2001 they held the first Art Basel in Miami Beach. Now, each December, Miami and Miami Beach become home to this one-of-a-kind art fair. The Miami Beach Convention Center serves as the main site for the fair. Across the causeway and on the mainland, we were able to position Miami's emerging neighborhoods as exciting places for art. This began to attract numerous other art fairs and enthusiasts to the city. Now, a number of events—everything from parties to exhibits to about twenty other art fairs—take place in Miami at the same time as the main fair.

Art Basel turned Miami into a capital of arts, with everybody from everywhere coming to Miami for the premier art event in the world. Now Basel finds itself thinking about how it can match the restaurants, great shows, and nightlife Miami has to offer. Now that fair goers have been to Miami, they want the same excitement in Basel. Art Basel propelled Miami into the arts stratosphere, and now Miami ranks among the top art destinations in the United States.

Our Miami Book Fair, run by Miami Dade College, was described by the *New York Times* as one of the great literary events in America. The Fair draws huge crowds from around the world to Downtown Miami, and is a key presentation point for major national and international authors wishing to expose their books. Miami Dade College also stepped in to operate another key event in Downtown Miami, the Miami Film Festival.

The Festival started in Miami in the early 1980s and then was moved out of the city when it came under the control of Florida International University (FIU). The president of FIU, Modesto Maidique, called me one day to tell me they were unable to continue funding the Festival, and would terminate it unless I could find someone to take over. I was very grateful he had contacted me because I could not let such an important festival die. I immediately called the president of Miami Dade

College, Eduardo Padrón. Since the college already was doing such a great job operating the Book Fair, it was time to add a Film Festival too. Eduardo agreed, and now the Festival is doing very well, serving among other things as a premiere showcase for Spanish language films, thanks in very large part to him.

Not only did we work to retain existing events, but we started to bring higher profile televised events to Miami, such as the MTV video music awards. We hosted the awards twice, setting the entire city abuzz. The MTV music awards brought the music industry into a city it already loved, and where many musicians already owned homes. It was natural for MTV to be here. In fact, Miami became the only city outside New York and Los Angeles to host the show.

We also hosted the Latin Grammys. The producers had attempted earlier to bring the show to Miami, but everyone had been unable to get past the issue that there might be performers from Cuba onstage. Because of that attitude, the show was being held in Los Angeles. I went out of my way to get the Latin Grammys to Miami. In the end no Cuban performers actually showed up, because they couldn't get entry visas. Still, we did have those who demonstrated (in a constitutional free speech area, which is fine). They should not, however, have been able to stop us from having the show at all, since the show was good for Miami: good for the city's image, and good for the city's economy.

▢ ▢ ▢

MAYORS CLEARLY UNDERSTAND the impact the arts have on a city. The history of many revitalized neighborhoods throughout America has centered around arts and artists moving in, providing a catalyst to neighborhoods, creation of economic activity and jobs, and a rise in property values. One of the clearest examples in Miami is the neighborhood surrounding our Performing Arts Center. Between 1996 and 2001, the Omni Community Redevelopment Area was underperforming in generating tax increment funds, created through increases in property values. Because nothing was being built in that area, property values were not increasing. The total taxable value increase during that period for the area had grown by only $40 million. In 2002, we broke ground on a new performing arts center. In the five years following, the total taxable value of the area grew by a billion dollars, all buoyed by an increase in the value of property around the Center. That is the kind of impact a facility like this can have on a neighborhood and on a city.

The $400 million for the Center came primarily from tax dollars paid by tourists as part of their room charge when they stayed in our hotels, along with some private contributions. Tourist dollars were reinvested and now generate more tourism. Local residents were not taxed. These projects pay for themselves, and Miami gained a world class Performing Arts Center. But we didn't stop there.

In 2004, a countywide referendum was held asking voters to approve funding for a multitude of projects totaling $2.9 billion. The question included several components such as housing, health facilities, streets, transportation, and so on. Fearing that the entire bond question would be defeated due to inclusion of money for the arts, county leaders decided to break the question into nine separate issues. Voters could choose to vote yes for funding one area, and no to another. Arts funding was the last question on the ballot. No one thought it was going to pass, especially with a price tag of $600 million.

I took it on myself to wage a campaign to get voters to say "yes" to arts funding. While Miami-Dade County leaders campaigned for the other bond questions, I focused on that. My staff didn't think this was politically wise, but I thought it was very important. It would mean funding for numerous cultural institutions including a new home for the Miami Science Museum and the Miami Art Museum in the downtown urban core. The voters said yes.

The economic impact on Miami of these projects is staggering, with new real estate development estimated at several billion dollars and tens of thousands of jobs. Moreover, the vibrancy created in the urban core by these projects led an Asian group to invest about half a billion dollars in that area with the view toward building a destination resort.

Arts clearly mean business. There aren't many communities that tax themselves $600 million to pay for the arts. But we did. Now, this decision is paying dividends. And that is something I am very proud of. When you see a television show, commercial, or movie that was filmed in Miami, it is difficult to imagine all the logistical issues that go into making those productions a reality. I was the first mayor of Miami to have an office dedicated specifically to facilitate production of film and television shows. Our office for Film, Arts, Culture, and Entertainment (FACE) became a one stop shop for television and film producers looking to shoot in Miami. Before this office was established, producers had to navigate the bureaucratic maze of City Hall (filming permits were issued by the Police Department, for example). The FACE office cleared all this up, helping filmmakers with matters from getting a permit to finding a place to screen dailies. Our office even partnered with the County and Miami Beach so that an application or inquiry into any one of these offices gave access to all the others. Filming throughout the entire geographical area is now made easier.

Our production friendly attitude helped Miami earn a place in the top ten rankings of the best places to film movies, according to *Moviemaker Magazine*. Productions in the City of Miami generated hundreds of millions of dollars for businesses throughout the city. Again, the arts mean business.

▢ ▢ ▢

HAVING SEEN THE impact of the arts on Miami and other cities, I think the federal government should make the arts a national priority. Before I became president of the U.S. Conference of Mayors, I was chair of the conference's arts committee (I had to resign the chair once I became president of the conference). Chairing that committee gave me an entirely new perspective on the arts, and gave me a platform to advocate for a cabinet level post for the arts—a secretary of the arts. It's something I still advocate. It's ridiculous to me that we lack someone at the national level who promotes tourism, arts, and culture.

An estimated one in eight people in the civilian work force have a job related to travel, tourism, arts, and culture. This sector has generated over 50 million jobs, more than $4 trillion in expenditures, $622 billion in taxes, and over $157 billion in trade surpluses. Not only is this one of the few trade surpluses we have, but most of the jobs in this sector cannot be shipped overseas. Studies have also shown that over 80 percent of traveling adults include historical and cultural activities in their itinerary, with 30 percent choosing their destination for travel based on these considerations. This industry is the nation's third largest employer behind health and business services. For Miami, this industry represents over $10 billion in expenditures directly supporting well over 100,000 jobs.

Think about it. When decisions are being made about tourism, arts, culture, who sits at the federal table speaking for these interests? We have an energy secretary, a homeland security secretary, an EPA director, a surgeon general, a drug czar, a manufacturing czar, and a trade representative—all charged with establishing policies, priorities, and objectives for our nation. Other countries throughout the world see the logic of a cabinet level position for arts, culture, and tourism: 66 percent of the countries in the Western Hemisphere have a cabinet level minister of tourism; 58 percent have ministers of culture and arts; 80 percent of European countries have a culture and arts minister. Yet the United States does not. It is time we show this industry the recognition and respect it deserves.

There is another, more transcendental reason to focus on the arts. It is the one piece of humanity that is outside time and ties us all together. Art is the soul and the spirit of each generation, to be passed along to the next and beyond. Through paintings, sculpture, books, architecture, music, and dance, we show our creativity, our expression, who we are—it is how we remain alive. Art connects us to the past, and is a legacy we leave for the future.

Consider this. We can walk into the Louvre and see a masterpiece by Da Vinci painted in the 1400s, walk into the Museum of Fine Arts in Boston and see a Greek vase and an Egyptian manuscript, sit at the Sydney Opera House and listen to beautiful music written in the 1800s. These opportunities did not exist in Miami—but they can now.

Conclusion

OF THE MANY memorable moments I had during my time as mayor, one of the most poignant came when I spoke at a naturalization ceremony in Miami. There were thousands of faces in that auditorium from all corners of the world, all with different backgrounds and stories. They were united by a common desire to become citizens of this great nation. On that day, out of many, we became one.

It was made more special by the fact that the ceremony was held in Miami, a city built on the aspirations and dreams of so many who have come to America searching for freedom and a better life. It is what this country gave my family, and what it gave me. I recalled to those at the ceremony how I came to the United States as a six-year-old on a freedom flight, sitting on my mother's lap, a political refugee fleeing a place where the government denies its people the freedoms and opportunities we cherish. We saw this country as so many others still do, as a beacon for hope, a land of boundless opportunity.

I spoke about how my mom and dad worked three jobs. They cleaned toilets, parked cars, washed dishes, and yet there was never despair. They knew that in America, if you work hard, you can give your children a better life. We lived in a clean, safe neighborhood. I went to a public school and enjoyed after-school activities. I worked as a school janitor making $1.10 an hour through a government program. Student loans made it possible for me to attend college and law school. At every turn of my life, especially in my youth, I benefited from a partnership. Because government invested in me, invested in the things needed to create opportunities, I was now speaking to these new citizens as the mayor of a major metropolitan city.

I couldn't help but to ask myself: Is this the same America I grew up in? Is this country still willing to provide the tools needed for advancement? Is America still willing to invest in its people? Does a six-year-old child today have the same access to opportunity that I did?

▢ ▢ ▢

DURING THE SUMMER prior to the 2008 presidential election, I was honored by my colleagues when they chose me to become the 66th president of the United States Conference of Mayors. It was a great honor in that I was not only the second Hispanic to lead the organization in its history, but that I also received recognition from fellow mayors of the work we did in Miami.

The Conference of Mayors is a nonpartisan group made up of mayors from 1,300 cities with populations of more than 30,000. It was organized on the night before President Franklin Delano Roosevelt's inauguration. Faced with the Great Depression and unemployment rates far worse than today's, a group of three mayors, including New York City mayor Fiorello La Guardia, convinced the federal government that the way out of the economic abyss was to direct federal investment to cities. This appeal turned into a $300 million influx into cities, ushering in the New Deal and helping lift the country out of the Great Depression.

As a student of history, I saw the similarities between that time and ours. In Miami, I was already starting to see the signs of an economic slowdown. Other mayors saw the same thing.

Before any presidential candidate or Beltway pundit figured out that the country was headed down a path toward economic disaster, we saw it and sounded the alarm. Mayors were the first to talk about our real estate and foreclosure crisis. We were first to connect this crisis to a much broader national economic emergency. We were first to call attention to the need to invest in our cities and our people. We saw that failure to do so would result in further economic stagnation and loss of competitive edge. At this rate we would fall farther and farther behind.

Then the Great Recession happened. Unemployment spiked, financial markets tanked, people began to lose their jobs, their homes, their savings. Banks stopped lending, businesses stopped investing, holding on to whatever cash and resources they could. Private spending stopped. The government had to step in. The answer: a renewed federal investment in cities.

Mayors came up with a plan for strategic targeted investment in five key areas: (1) increasing public safety; (2) improving economic opportunity (by alleviating poverty, better education, access to housing, meaningful health care reform); (3) improving infrastructure; (4) preserving our environment; and (5) fostering arts and tourism. We would rebuild America by rebuilding our cities. We presented this plan to both presidential candidates. The difference became that while past leaders in Washington listened to mayors, current ones did not.

◻ ◻ ◻

WHY INVEST IN CITIES?

Metro areas are driving the national economy, accounting for 92 percent of the nation's economic growth, almost 90 percent of all jobs, income, and Gross Domestic Product. Mayors are the first responders and front line of American politics. We are adept at problem solving, finding solutions, even with strained budgets. We don't print money like they do in D.C., but we balance our budgets every year. When people have a problem, it's not the president who gets a phone call; it's not the vice president, or a member of the cabinet. It's one of us. The phone rings and the buck stops on the mayor's desk. If we make an unpopular decision, we can't get on a plane and head back to the safety of the Beltway or a state capital; we'll get stopped at the gas station or the corner store. Mayors are closest to the people, and most aware of their needs.

So we all came together from across the political spectrum, every party, every size city, every region of the country: we all agreed on this course of action. But what did we get from Washington? Rather than a targeted investment in America's infrastructure, we got a stimulus bill. It was a laundry list stuffed with pet projects to satisfy the political constituencies of every member of Congress powerful enough to direct appropriations into their districts. This is how we do it in America.

Money and investments are allocated not based on need or priority, but by rank and seniority in Congress. If there is a bridge in your city that is falling apart, but you happen to be a junior member of Congress, or worse yet from the wrong party, too bad. It is unlikely you will get any money. If you've been in Congress forever and have risen through the ranks to become one of the appropriation "Cardinals," or better yet, the appropriations chair, well then, you can get a bridge to nowhere. You can also give "bridges to nowhere" and other goodies to all your political allies. Both sides are guilty of this nonsense. This isn't targeted investment--it is plain wasteful spending. It's also an abdication of responsibility, and a massive failure to lead.

⌑ ⌑ ⌑

WASHINGTON HAS LOST its sense of purpose, no longer investing in our cities or in our people. Plain and simple, it has abandoned cities, engaging in endless bickering while people throughout this country suffer. Let us briefly look at the state of our union with respect to these key areas:

Expanding economic opportunity and education

❏ Over 60 percent of America's children don't read or perform math at grade level; the number is higher for minorities. In our largest cities, over 50 percent of children don't make it past high school.

❏ Over half of America's children live in poverty or are classified as low income—the numbers are higher for minorities.

❏ Close to 10 million children in this country have no health insurance. Many middle class Americans are one paycheck, one sickness away from economic catastrophe.

❏ 35 million Americans go hungry, including nearly 13 million children.

❏ Americans are being priced out of their homes or losing their homes at alarming rates—and the number of homeless is still at unacceptable levels.

❏ 12 million students will drop out over the course of the next decade, resulting in a loss to the nation's economy of $3 trillion.

Public safety

❏ We see violence increase in our cities, and there are more gang members than there are police officers.

❏ Today, we have fewer police on the streets than before 9/11.

❏ Youth violence accounts for 20 percent of all violence and is the second leading cause of death among our youth. Well over half of homicides in America involve people under 29 years old. Our next generation is killing each other.

❏ We have the highest incarceration rate in the world.

❏ If you are a young black man, you have a 1 in 3 chance of going to jail, 1 in 4 if you are Latino.

❏ It is now cheaper to purchase an AK-47 Soviet assault rifle than a video game console on inner city streets.

Infrastructure investments

☐ According to a report by the American Society of Civil Engineers, $2.2 trillion needs to be invested over five years to bring the condition of the nation's infrastructure up to a good condition.

☐ The number of deficient dams has risen to more than 4,000, including almost 2,000 high hazard dams. There are more than 85,000 dams in the U.S., and the average age is just over 51 years.

☐ Leaking pipes lose an estimated seven billion gallons of clean drinking water a day. Cities are losing 5–40 percent of their clean drinking water.

☐ More than 85 percent of the nation's estimated 100,000 miles of levees (remember New Orleans) are locally owned and maintained. Many of them are over 50 years old and were originally built to protect crops from flooding.

☐ Aging systems discharge billions of gallons of untreated wastewater into U.S. surface waters each year.

☐ We spend 4.2 billion hours a year stuck in traffic (time that can instead be spent with our families) at a cost of to the economy of $78.2 billion, or $710 per motorist.

☐ Congestion on our roads costs us $70 to 78 billion in wasted fuel. Freight bottlenecks waste $200 billion a year in inefficiency.

☐ 50 percent of our navigable waterways are functionally obsolete.

☐ More than 26 percent—more than 1 in 4—of the nation's bridges are structurally deficient or functionally obsolete.

☐ According to a survey of mayors, 35 percent of cities don't know where their water supplies will come from in 20 years.

☐ Most of these water projects (95–98 percent) are funded by local governments. Water and sewer is the second highest category of government spending next to public education.

❒ The United States invented the Internet, but we now rank 15 in the world in broadband adoption. South Korea, Japan, Canada, Spain, and Poland surpass us.

❒ In ten years, 70 percent of all jobs will require technology knowledge and skills.

Sustainability through design and urban planning

❒ The United States still has no energy policy.

❒ Gasoline continues to hover at $3 to $4 a gallon. Americans spend $2.7 billion per day on their cars. That's over $80 billion per month. This is quite a stimulus program we have established for foreign (often hostile) nations.

❒ Demand for electricity has grown by 25 percent since 1990.

❒ While public transportation saves 1.4 billion gallons of fuel each year, we continue to pour money into expanding and building new highways.

❒ Public transportation also saves the average U.S household up to $6,200 a year in transportation costs. Proximity to public transit options determines use. Yet, only 5 percent of commuters take public transit due to lack of access.

❒ Our addiction to foreign oil has us borrowing money from unfriendly governments to buy oil from other unfriendly governments, in what is called the greatest transfer of wealth in history, $700 billion a year.

Fostering arts, culture, travel, and tourism

❒ The United States has no national policy on arts, culture, travel, and tourism.

❒ Travel is America's leading service sector generating over $100 billion from international travelers.

- Security measures have caused U.S. airports to be seen as "unfriendly," with a drop of travelers to the U.S., leading to a loss of 250,000 jobs.
- The FAA has stated that airport delays cost our economy more than $10 billion.
- While the travel market has expanded worldwide, the U.S. share has declined 35 percent over the past 15 years.
- President Obama signed the Travel Promotion Act in 2010 to reverse some of this decline. Amount of federal investment made? $0.
- The National Endowment for the Arts received a little over $150 million from Congress in FY 2011 in a multi-trillion dollar budget.

What is the federal government's reaction to all this? Is it outrage? Is it anger? Is it a call to arms? No. People in Washington just don't talk about it. To them, these are all "local" issues. Instead, we get debates on gay marriage, abortion, illegal immigrants and the border, gun control, the conspiracy of global warming, and eliminating the "evil" Environmental Protection Agency. They fight for the distinction of who among them "loves" the middle class more, and who would you rather sit down and have a beer with.

Once in office, Beltway politicans cut funds to local governments, while pushing down more and more responsibility. Cuts to community development block grants, cuts to affordable housing, cuts to public safety, cuts in education, job training, arts, infrastructure—these investments in our cities and our people, all cut. Mayors are then left to find solutions.

When faced with inaction on climate change, it was former Seattle mayor Greg Nickels who brought over 1,000 mayors together under a Climate Action Plan to in effect implement the Kyoto Protocol throughout our nation's cities. Former Chicago mayor Richard Daley and former Austin mayor Will Wynn showed the nation that you can have economic development and an environmental conscience. When illegal guns and assault weapons flooded city streets, and the federal government let the assault weapons ban expire, New York mayor Michael Bloomberg and Boston mayor Tom Menino raised their voices against violence in our cities. Faced with cuts to federal programs that help the most vulnerable, mayors like Los Angeles mayor Antonio Villaraigosa took poverty reduction head on. While the federal government claims to "leave no child behind," we all know better, which is why mayors like Mike Coleman in Columbus and former Atlanta mayor Shirley Franklin developed education policies that put children first. While Congress gives us multi-million-dollar bridges to nowhere, former Denver mayor (and now Colorado governor) John Hickenlooper brought common sense to infrastructure.

Mayors throughout America are the government of first resort. They have also become the government of last resort.

☐ ☐ ☐

IN THE YEARS since mayors gathered to create a plan of investment for our nation, the country is still lagging economically and in every other indicator. Why?

Leadership has been replaced by partisanship. Statesmen have been replaced with strategists and pollsters. Professional, objective journalists have been replaced with partisan pundits and bloggers. Republicans and Democrats are playing a game where the aim is to score points, win the news cycle, embarrass your opponents, and hold on to power. This constant battle is threatening to reverse all of the progress that has been made on the things that make America great. It's also paralyzing our ability to get things done.

Consider that in 2011, our nation was paralyzed because congressional leaders and the president could not agree on an increase in the nation's debt ceiling, causing the United States to lose its perfect credit rating for the first time in the country's history. Our country is running on a budget extended by "continuing resolutions" because Congress and the president can't adopt a budget, much less balance one. Politics today is not a battle between grand ideas, but about bumper sticker sound bites. Politicians actually believe the electorate is too ignorant or too disinterested to pay attention to anything that is remotely new, remotely bold, or remotely thoughtful.

Ideas in Washington are polar opposites. One side wants to spend our way out of everything. The other side wants to spend nothing at all. Even the simplest idea is shot down as too expensive, or not expensive enough. Both sides are terribly wrong. The fighting over extreme positions that focus on the "haves" and "have nots" have caused the abandonment of traditional centrist and practical policies, and ignoring the middle class.

The funny thing is that Republicans and Democrats used to agree on the goals for America. They disagreed on how to get there, but progress was made. President Ronald Reagan, a Republican, worked with speaker Tip O'Neill, a Democrat, to get things done. President Bill Clinton, a Democrat, worked with the Republican-controlled House of Representatives. They disagreed on many things. But they all got around a table and got things done. Even on issues like the environment, where such a wide divide exists, there was always ground for agreement. Many people forget that it was a Republican president, Richard Nixon, who started the EPA and helped pass the Clean Air and Water Acts. Incidentally, it was also Nixon who started providing Community Development Block Grants to cities, a program that Presidents George W. Bush and Barack Obama have severely cut funding for. Now, we have gone beyond any agreement. The point is to disagree.

If the Democrats propose something, Republicans call it pork. If the Republicans propose something, Democrats call it draconian. How many times have we heard the same stale talking points repeated over and over from both sides? Republicans say "Democrats are increasing the deficit." Democrats say "Republicans want tax cuts for the rich." Sound familiar?

The echo-chamber that envelops the Beltway bounces with the same tired platitudes and recycled talking points from both sides. It has become so predictable that before pundits even open their mouth, you can be 99 percent sure what they are going to say depending on whether there is an "R" or a "D" next to their name. The aim is to win the day's news cycle, win the next election, and crush the opposition. Those in the media have stopped being journalists and reporters, but are now cheerleaders, taking sides and distorting the news and facts all to achieve their ends. If all you do is watch Fox News or MSNBC, your intransigence will grow even farther. Information that used to be verified and analyzed by professional and respected journalists (think of Cronkite, Murrow, and the like) is now blogged, tweeted, and disseminated 24 hours a day, often unchecked, a never ending flow of "gotcha" and armchair criticism that stifles serious thought and debate. The national political process has become a shouting match, and the shouting has drowned out common sense.

No one I know favors pollution, people getting sick, endless traffic, and addiction to foreign oil. There is not a single Democrat or Republican that will tell me "I want children to be illiterate," or "I like it when bridges fall apart..." So why has it become so difficult to agree? Why is it so difficult to get anything done? This inaction is endemic in the political system. While people are suffering and looking for leadership and solutions, neither party is offering them. You name a single issue this country faces today—and there are many—and both sides are entrenched, guided by ideology and intransigence rather than principle and just good old fashioned common sense.

A poll was released in 2011 in which disapproval ratings for Democrats went up 7 points versus 20 points for Republicans. The headline was: "Democrats Out Message Republicans." Out message? Are you kidding me? Both were viewed more negatively! It just meant that people hated one party a little less. Don't vote for me because I'm good, vote for me because the other guy is worse. This is a race to the bottom. No one any more has the courage to lead. Is this the best we can do?

🗅 🗅 🗅

INSTEAD OF OUT messaging each other, how about we find some solutions? Some people tell me the political system is broken beyond repair. They've lost hope in politics and politicians. I say it's not true. Look in your cities—in your local communities—look at what your mayors are doing together with all of you, and there you will find the solution to this nation's problems. Much in the same way Miami was able to rise again through leadership and investment, so can our nation. It is happening every day in our cities, in spite of the rudderless Beltway leaders. Imagine how much more we could all do if mayors could count on our partners in the federal government for cooperation and not obstruction or inaction.

When I met with both candidates during the 2008 presidential election and they asked my advice, I told them: run for mayor of the United States. It is the same advice I would give to all future presidential candidates. Mayors know that problems are not right or left, liberal or conservative—they are challenges that we must all face and solve together. We need to be pragmatic and practical, just like in business. Look for areas where we can agree, and move forward. Work on the things we all agree on.

I read the following statement in a paper on climate change, but it is adaptable to every single issue we now face:

> The climate wars will no doubt continue between extremes on both sides, but that should not delay a far-larger set of pragmatic Americans from embracing policies and measures that attract widespread agreement, are adjustable over time, incremental in

their implementation, and provide positive feedbacks for further action.

For too long, the national and international climate debate has been little more than that: a debate. There is much that people and nations can agree to disagree on, even as they agree to work together on practical actions. It is time to get started.

It is indeed time to get started. Our nation is far too great, far too promising to have its future left up to the whims of politicians whose only interest is in winning the next election. It is time to get started—and it starts with all of us.

▢ ▢ ▢

ONE FINAL THOUGHT. Some would argue that when times are tough and the economy is slow, it is a time to scale back; that we should not invest to create jobs and prosperity; that we should not grow. Do we heed these words of fear and doubt? Should we retreat? Should I have to tell my children about the days when the United States was great? That as a nation we settled for good enough? Or, do we challenge ourselves and continue to move forward?

To me the choice is clear. While there is no doubt that these are difficult economic times, we cannot lose faith in our country, we cannot fail to invest in the promise it has always offered. We cannot sit idly and let the world pass us by. When these voices of doubt say we should not or cannot—we must answer, why not?

Government investment is not about a vision: it is a mandate—it is why government exists. Our most solemn duty is to leave a country where poverty is not a lifelong sentence, but a temporary condition to be overcome. A country that combines economic prosperity with environmental sustainability, where our children can receive the best education, afford a home, hold a good paying job, have access to the arts, and live in well-planned communities. We must leave a nation much greater than the one left to us. We must accept the challenge to fulfill this duty.

To echo the words uttered by a U.S. president not so long ago: in the final analysis, our most basic common link is that we all inhabit this nation together—we all breathe the same air, we all cherish our children's future, and we are all mortal.

Index

Acknowledgments

LOVE AND HONOR your family. Through good times and bad, they will be your one constant source of support and strength.

Cherish your friends. It is the quality of your friendships and not the number of friends that will matter most in your life. Always be there for them. They will be there for you.

Surround yourself with good people. No matter how smart you think you are, no matter your own sense of worth, no matter your chosen path in life: without the helping hand of others, you will not reach your full potential.

During our youth, most of us heard these and other pearls of wisdom from our parents, grandparents, teachers, coaches, and others. Although we may not have fully appreciated their significance then, there is no question that they become an integral part of our value system, and the older we get, the more we recognize their worth.

I have been blessed with a great family, wonderful friends, and some really exceptionally good people. Words cannot fully express my gratitude to the hundreds of individuals who helped shape my life. Undoubtedly, I will omit many of their names here. I deeply apologize to you.

First, my family. You will read about them in this book. My parents, Manolo and Elisa Diaz, and my grandparents, Benigno and Hortensia Galnares, and my parents only sibling, my uncle Benigno and my aunt Aida. My brother Jorge and my cousins, Lena, Julio, Alex, Lysis, Luis and Marlen. My children, Manny (and my wonderful daughter-in-law, Stephanie), Natalie, Bobby, and Elisa. My grandchildren Colin, Gavin, and Manny. And, of course, the very special person in my life, my wife, Robin Smith Diaz.

I wrote this book with Ignacio Ortiz-Petit. Throughout my term, Ignacio helped to shape my messages and ideas. An extremely gifted writer, he would turn those grand ideas into words of action and inspiration. In the process, we became good friends. Bill Finan, my editor at the University of Pennsylvania Press, also deserves my heartfelt thanks for his invaluable assistance in the writing of this book.

From the little league playing fields through today, I have been blessed with lasting friendships. My Belen Jesuit High School graduating class: George Aguilera, Frank Aparicio, Raul Aparicio, Donato Arguelles, Abelardo Blanco, Luis Bulas, Jorge Campaña, Antolín Cossio, Mike Crudele, Raul Davalos, Julio Fernandez, Alfredo Fernandez de Castro, Alfonso Forment, Idelfonso Fuentes, Luis Fuentes, Prudencio Garcia, Ramon Garcia, Jose Gutiérrez, Armando Incera, Jorge Lopez, Rene Lamar, Juan Marrero, Luis Martinez, Andy Mejides, Mickey Miñagorri, Luis Navia, Gustavo Padron, Carlos Penin, Henry Pfister, Pedro Pina, Carlos Reyes, Antonio Ricol, Luis Rivero, Paul Rodriguez, Joaquín Ruhi, Mario Ruiz de la Torre, Miguel Ruiz, Paco Ruiz, Enrique Sanchez, Luis Santamarina, Jorge Smith, Charles Stock, and Carlos Valdes.

Others from Belen played or continue to play a significant role in my life. The faculty members who inspired me to learn and constantly challenged me to be an independent thinker: Father Jose Izquierdo, Father Luis Ripoll, Jimmy Perez, Carlos Barquin, Patrick Collins, and Mariano Loret de Mola. For the past 35 years, Mariano has served as the inspirational leader, mentor, coach, disciplinarian, and second father to so many of us. He helped an entire generation of young boys, myself included, learn to become men.

In addition to my former classmates, I would also like to acknowledge numerous other members of the Belen family: Percy Aguila, Alberto Aran, Fernando Aran, Jorge Cabrera, Cesar Conde, Vicente Cossio, Ernesto de la Fe, Manuel Dominguez, Tony Ferrer, Jose Garrido, Sergio Gonzalez, Carlos Fernandez Guzman, Timothy Harrington, Jorge Hernandez Toraño, Ricardo Ibarria, Ruben Marrero, Pedro Mencia, Manuel Morales, Luis Perez, Justo Luis Pozo, Alex Puente, Orlando Puente, Frankie Ruiz, Henry Sori, Frank Quintero, Gerardo Simms, and Pedro Torres.

Professionally, I have been blessed with terrific law partners, including Jeffrey Berkowitz, Richard Berkowitz, Kendall Coffey, Rolando Delgado, Carlos de Zayas, Eduardo Garcia, Richard Lydecker, and Juan T. O'Naghten.

Through the years I have had the opportunity to work with the staff of many elected officials. My staff is by the far the best I have ever come across. My chiefs of staff: Javier Fernandez, Francois Illas, Jose Mallea, and Suzanna Valdez. My Dream Team also consisted of Vivianne Bohorques, Otto Boudet, Gustavo Chacon, Isabel de Armas, Isabel de Quesada, Marcelino Feal, Steven Ferreiro, David Fry, Anthony Georges Pierre, Irain Gonzalez, Danny Hanlon, Linda Haskins, Mayto Igualdad, Jesse Manzano, Lisa Martinez, Alejandro Miyar, Jeffrey Mondesir, Kathryn Moore, Justin O'Brien, Ignacio Ortiz-Petit, Kelly Penton, Fatima Perez, Lisette Perna, Lazara Pinera, Helena Poleo, Michelle Spence Jones, Marjory St. Elien, Samaki Variety, and Armando Villaboy. I am also very grateful to the police officers who were assigned to me: Fernando Acosta and Robert Rodriguez. When I reflect on all that was accomplished, I am amazed that our entire office staff never exceeded 14 people at any one time during my eight years in office.

I am also deeply grateful to a city staff that believed in my vision for Miami and brought with them an unprecedented "can-do" attitude.

My city managers: Joe Arriola, Carlos Giménez, and Pete Hernandez. The department directors: Ola Aluko, Kelly Barkett, Laura Bilberry, Otto Boudet, LeeAnn Brehm, William Bryson, Ernest Burkeen, Pete Chircut, Ana Gelabert Sanchez, Barbara Gomez, Diana Gomez, Ricardo Gonzalez, Linda Haskins, Maurice Kemp, Peter Korinis, Hector Lima, Mariano Loret de Mola, Glenn Marcos, Rosalie Mark, Alex Martinez, Carlos McDonald, George Mensah, Trish Mindingall, Clarence Patterson, Kelly Penton, Don Riedel, David Rosemond, Robert Ruano, Lourdes Slayzyk, Mario Soldevilla, Larry Spring, John Timoney, and Kathleen Woods Richardson.

Others in city government that deserve mention, including: Robert Fenton, Frank Fernandez, Natalie French, Luciana Gonzalez, Francis Mitchell, Stuart Myers, Ricardo Novas, Cesar Nuñez, Frank Novell, Jim Osteen, Juan Pascual, Danette Perez, Jorge R. Perez, William Porro, Mario Riquelme and Jorge Soliño.

I could not possibly list the names of all city employees. But they should know this: that I am grateful for their public service, proud of what we accomplished together, and honored to have been a part of the Miami family. Thank you for sharing in my journey.

And, of course, I was blessed with an outstanding and dedicated group of City Commissioners: Angel Gonzalez, Linda Haskins, Joe Sanchez, Marc Sarnoff, Michelle Spence Jones, the late Arthur E. Teele, Jr., and Johnny Winton. They were true partners in the city's transformation, and along the way, we became friends.

Other special friends and supporters include: Mike Abrams, Jose Abreu, Al Armada, Loreta Armada, Julio Avello, Maria Cristina Barros, Esteban Bencomo, Migdalia Bencomo, George Burgess, Antonio Cabrera, Judge Gisela Cardonne Ely, Alberto Carvalho, Joe Cayre, Paul Cejas, Armando Codina, Rudy Crew, Simon Cruz, Steve Dunfey, the late Judge Margarita Esquiroz, Emilio Estefan, Gloria Estefan, Esther Favole, Jorge Fernandez, Judge Mario Goderich, Joey Goldman, Tony Goldman, Seth Gordon, Julie Grimes, Tony Grippa, Matthew Haggman, Dean Jeannette Hausler, Daniel Herman, Alberto Ibarguen, Neisen Kasdin, Judge Maria Korvick, Luis Lauredo, Danet Linares, Alberto Lorenzo, Charley Lydecker, Alfredo Mesa, Julian Mesa, Pete Mitchell, Nitin Motwani, Senator Bill Nelson, Brian Nelson, Mike O'Donovan, Alan Ojeda, President Eduardo Padron, Sergio Penton, Jorge Perez, Luis Perna, Daniel Pfeffer, Elizabeth Plater-Zyberk, Luis Reiter, Craig Robins, Ileana Romeu, President Mark Rosenberg, Barry Rush, David Samson, Steve Schwarzberg, President Donna Shalala, Javier Soto, John Stack, and Mark Van Fossam.

I am eternally grateful to two very special friends and supporters: University of Pennsylvania Professors Eugenie L. Birch and Susan M. Wachter. Without their encouragement, commitment, and support, this book would have never been written.

My years with the United States Conference of Mayors gave me the opportunity to work with some of the greatest elected officials in the United States. My colleagues served as my mentors and my inspiration for many of our initiatives. I had the privilege and honor of working closely with Jerry Abramson (Louisville; now Lieutenant Governor of Kentucky), Mike Bloomberg (New York City), David Cicilline (Providence; now a member of Congress), Michael Coleman (Columbus), Frank Cownie (Des Moines), Richard M. Daley (Chicago), Ron Dellums (Oakland), Robert Duffy (Rochester; now Lieutenant Governor of New York), Bob Foster (Long Beach), Shirley Franklin (Atlanta), Jim Garner (Hempstead), the late Mike Guido (Dearborn), John Hickenlooper (Denver; now Governor of Colorado), Kevin Johnson (Sacramento), Elizabeth Kautz (Burnsville), Dannel Malloy (Stamford; now Governor of Connecticut), Marc Morial (New Orleans), Thomas Menino (Boston), Arlene Mulder (Arlington Heights), Gavin Newsom (San Francisco; now Lieutenant Governor of California), Greg Nickels (Seattle), Michael Nutter (Philadelphia), Martin O'Malley (Baltimore; now Governor of Maryland), Beverly O'Neill (Long Beach), Doug Palmer (Trenton), Don Plusquellic (Akron), Miguel Pulido (Santa Ana), Bill Purcell (Nashville),

Joseph Riley (Charleston), Raul Salinas (Laredo), Scott Smith (Mesa), Antonio Villaraigosa (Los Angeles), and Wellington Webb (Denver).

Working with the Conference of Mayors leadership and staff, I was proud to promote the placement of several Florida mayors to positions of leadership. I believe that the seven Florida mayors in the Conference of Mayors leadership represent the largest group from any state. They are Juan Carlos Bermudez (Doral), Alvin Brown (Jacksonville), Joy Cooper (Hallandale Beach), Buddy Dyer (Orlando), John Marks (Tallahassee), Lori Moseley (Miramar), and Frank Ortis (Pembroke Pines).

Finally, the success of the U.S. Conference of Mayors depends to a very large extent on the hard work and total dedication of a long-serving staff led by its Chief Executive Officer and Executive Director of over 30 years, Tom Cochran. Tom is passionate about the role of cities and America's Mayors are his extended family. May God continue to bless Tom, his family and his dedicated staff.

CPSIA information can be obtained at www.ICGtesting.com
Printed in the USA
LVOW040835121212

311299LV00002B/5/P